Buy It, Sell It,
MAKE MONEY

Buy It, Sell It,
MAKE MONEY

Your Guide to Finding and Reselling
Luxury Goods for Personal Wealth

Daren and Nancy Baughman

iUniverse, Inc.
New York Lincoln Shanghai

Buy It, Sell It, MAKE MONEY
Your Guide to Finding and Reselling Luxury Goods for Personal Wealth

iUniverse books may be ordered through booksellers or by contacting:

iUniverse
2021 Pine Lake Road, Suite 100
Lincoln, NE 68512
www.iuniverse.com
1-800-Authors (1-800-288-4677)

Because of the dynamic nature of the Internet, any Web addresses or links contained in this book may have changed since publication and may no longer be valid.

ISBN: 978-0-595-42689-8 (pbk)
ISBN: 978-0-595-68178-5 (cloth)
ISBN: 978-0-595-87020-2 (ebk)

Printed in the United States of America

Buy It, Sell It, Make Money is in no way authorized by, affiliated with, or endorsed by any product or service provider mentioned in the book. All references to eBay and other trademarked properties are used in accordance with the fair use doctrine and are not meant to imply that this book is an eBay product for advertising or other commercial purposes.

Readers who employ the Flipster System do so at their own risk. The resale trade and auctions are unpredictable by their very natures. The authors and publishers of this book cannot guarantee financial success and therefore disclaim any liability, loss, or risk sustained as a result of using the information given in this book.

The information, ideas, and suggestions in this book are not intended to render legal advice. Before following any suggestions contained in this book, readers should consult their personal attorneys. Neither the authors nor the publisher shall be liable or responsible for any loss or damage allegedly arising as a consequence of the use or application of any information or suggestion in this book.

Contents

Introduction

The family car pulled into the muddy parking lot of the rural Pennsylvania auction house in late September 1978. The corn in the field next to the parking lot was high and brown, waiting for the farmer to pick the last ears before winter. Two boys dashed out of the car and ran to the lines of boxes that had been set outside the auction house. The good items were stacked neatly on tables inside, but the junky items were placed outside the auction house where they would later be sold in box lots. The oldest boy, who was thirteen at the time, picked through the old tools and household items trying to find something of interest. On his allowance, he could not afford anything inside the auction house, but occasionally he would find an old pocketknife or toy car outside that he would buy.

The boy spotted a large box overflowing with jewelry. The jewelry box was made of flimsy cardboard covered with cloth, and the hinges were broken so it would not have stayed open except for the mass of jewelry that was pouring out the top. Piled inside the box was a twisted mix of plastic necklaces and broken chains, which the boy pulled out in one large, tangled lump. Deeper inside the box were clouded rhinestone brooches and random earrings with rusted screw-on backs. As he searched around in the box, the boy pulled out a gold, leaf-shaped brooch with a clear stone in the center. He could tell it was better than all the other jewelry in the box, and when he turned over the piece he saw it was marked "14kt" on the back. The boy's mother had taught him about gold marks so he knew the brooch was most likely worth something. How much it was worth? He was not sure.

The auctioneer started walking beside the line of boxes, auctioning off one at a time. When he came to the box of jewelry, the boy raised his hand to bid. The old-timers at the auction house teased the boy about buying this box of jewelry for a girlfriend. Wisely the boy kept silent about the prize that lay at the bottom of the box and was able to purchase the entire box lot for fifty cents.

After the family arrived back home, the boy showed his parents the leaf-shaped brooch. The brooch was indeed fourteen-karat gold, and the clear center stone was a nice quarter-carat diamond. The brooch was worth approximately $200 at the time. The little boy tried to give the brooch to his mother, but she said that, since he'd purchased it with his own money, she would buy it from him. The mother paid her son $50 for the diamond brooch.

The diamond brooch that caused Daren's "light bulb" moment

At the age of thirteen, the boy was ecstatic—he had turned fifty cents into $50 just by knowing the value of something. That was what Daren Baughman, my husband, calls his "light bulb" moment. He suddenly realized that knowledge meant money and that using his knowledge to buy and resell goods would be an easy and legal way to make money.

That is the information we would like to impart to you.

Shortly after discovering the brooch, Daren began to work part-time at the auction house as a runner. A runner is the person who holds up the current item up for auction and then gives it to the winning bidder. There, Daren began his resale career in earnest. He purchased items at the auction house—such as guitars, electronics, and toys—that he knew he could resell at school for a profit. An entrepreneur was born!

Flash forward to the year 1993. Daren and I had been dating several months, and I needed to install a fence around the backyard of my newly purchased home. Daren and my father decided to put up the fence, but we needed lumber. Daren and I went out to purchase the building materials at a local hardware store, which was going out of business. We went to the back desk. I told the gentleman what I needed, and he gave me the price. I automatically agreed to take the building materials at the price that was quoted.

Luckily Daren jumped in and started to negotiate the price of the lumber. Since the hardware store was going out of business and was trying to liquidate the inventory, Daren was able to negotiate 40 percent off the retail price by agreeing to take all of the fence posts and sections they had in stock, which, as it turned out, was only a few more pieces than I'd planned to buy anyway. I remembered being very impressed with my new boyfriend, so impressed in fact that I married him a year later. Until that day, I had never thought about trying to negotiate a deal with a retail store. I had gone to flea markets and antique stores to barter with dealers, but I had never tried to take that skill outside those small venues.

Since that time, Daren and I have each developed our purchasing and negotiation skills to the point that they are second nature to us, and those skills are a huge part of our lives. Daren is a certified and licensed auctioneer and a personal property appraiser. He has worked full-time in corporate procurement for over seventeen years, and he holds a certificate in Procurement and Material Management and a Certified Purchasing Manager Designation through the Institute for Supply Management. I am a Certified Property Appraiser with the Certified Appraisers Guild. I work full-time as an appraiser as well as own and operate our business, eBizAuctions has been featured in *Entrepreneur Magazine* twice and in a local, syndicated newspaper article. Before I started eBizAuctions, I had ten years experience as a financial analyst with a large fortune 500 company.

Daren and I would like to introduce you to the amazing and profitable world of Frugal Luxury Investment Purchasing or, as we will refer to it, the Flipster System. The Flipster System will open the door for you to be able to purchase high-quality, luxury goods that you never thought possible. Not every person has the ability or desire to run a million-dollar company or earn a six-figure paycheck, but everyone would like to have the financial means to purchase items that are important to them. Daren and I have been running our resale company, eBizAuctions, for over four years. We have collected hundreds of luxury goods for ourselves and have sold thousands of items for profit.

There are hundreds of books, seminars, and infomercials that promise to teach you how to earn millions of dollars overnight, but these fall short in reality. Most people cannot follow the complicated plans set out in these get-rich-quick schemes, and most people cannot leave their full-time jobs to pursue such ill-fated dreams. Did you ever wonder why someone who supposedly is making millions of dollars by using a "system" would bother to write a book teaching others how to do it? It takes months and months to write a book and even more time to promote it. If I was making millions of dollars every year, I would not be writing a book. I would spend my time making millions of dollars or enjoying the millions. If something does not make sense and is not logical, then it is usually not true. I cannot make you an overnight millionaire, but I can and will show you how to make extra money. We want to show you how to increase your buying power so that you'll have extra income to ease financial burdens and allow you to enjoy the finer things in life.

We will show you how to get the things you really want in life without having a high-powered job or million-dollar pay check. I do not want to run a large business. I like what I do as an appraiser and seller of antiques and collectibles. I value my free time, and I do not want to deal with the pressures and time commitment that a big operation would require. I think that, especially in America, there is too much pressure to be wealthy and not enough emphasis on living a happy and fulfilling life. In this book, we would like to share with you our Flipster System and our philosophy, so you can have everything you want and still have the free time to enjoy those items.

In this book, we will reveal to you the secrets that we and our family have used for the past forty years to acquire luxury goods. We will help you in your quest to purchase all the luxury items you have dreamed of owning. We will also teach you how to resell goods for profit so you can have the financial freedom to live the life that you want to live.

The fundamental Flipster philosophy is that *it is not important how much money you earn but how you choose to spend it.* We will teach you how to spend wisely and, thus, increase your buying power so that, no matter how much money you earn, you will have the ability to enjoy all the things in life that are important to you.

We will provide you with real-life examples of how we have paid pennies on the dollar for both new and secondhand name-brand goods. We will teach you how and when to negotiate. We will provide you with a guide to the best brands to purchase. We will also provide you with secret places to purchase high-end goods.

This book is not about clipping coupons to save twenty cents on a bottle of ketchup. It's about how to purchase a $3000 stereo for $250 or a $4,000 diamond ring for $600. We will teach you how and when to trade up your current goods so you can buy newer and better goods without going broke. We will teach you how to buy name-brand, designer clothes so you will be better dressed than your boss. This book will teach you how to intelligently purchase the things that are negotiable so you will have the money to pay for the things in life that are nonnegotiable. It will also teach you a powerful way to live life richly without having a huge paycheck.

Anyone can learn to be a Flipster! Daren has a great foundation built on years of experience working at auction houses, but I had no such experience. Daren showed me how to buy the right types of items and how to negotiate a great deal so that we could resell items at amazing profits. We have written this book to make it easy to train yourself how to be a Flipster. The sourcing guide and field guide will make the learning process go smoothly and will keep you from making costly mistakes. We have condensed years of experience into one book so that, within a few short weeks, anyone can flip everyday and luxury goods for resale. There are great deals to be had all over America, and we cannot possibly get to them all, so we want to teach others our system.

Chapter One
F is for Frugal

Frugal adj: avoiding waste[1]

BE FRUGAL; BUY SMART; LIVE IN LUXURY

To many people, the above statement appears to contradict itself; but it does not. How can one be frugal and yet live in luxury? The word frugal paints a picture of Ebenezer Scrooge hovering over a tiny bit of coal in his freezing office and counting pennies until late in the night. To us, frugal people are clever, restraining, and prudent in their buying habits so that they can afford the things in life that are important to them.

I know a person who only uses ten-watt light bulbs in his home and has thick, heavy curtains that he keeps closed all summer to keep out the heat. While I have no doubt that he may save a few pennies each year on his electric bill, I think this is a little foolish. First, the amount that an average home would save by switching from one hundred-watt bulbs to ten-watt bulbs is nominal. Second, with the low lights and closed curtains, the house is dark and depressing. I do not want to live that way! It would make much more sense to invest in the newer, more efficient bulbs, electrical appliances, and home insulation than to make a virtually useless sacrifice like using ten-watt light bulbs.

To the casual observer looking in on our lives, Daren and I would seem anything but frugal. But that would be a misconception. We may live in a custom-designed, four thousand-square-foot home with quality furnishings. We may dress in name brand clothing, drive nice vehicles, and take great vacations every year. But we are very frugal. We live richer lives than most people who have twice as much income as we do, and we do so by being frugal and buying smart.

Living frugally means that sometimes you have to delay your purchases. For example, there is a certain designer who makes clothing I like that fits me well. The retail prices at this store are more than I choose to pay, so I have to wait for a bargain. Note that I wrote *choose to pay*. I could afford to purchase clothing at this designer store, but paying full price would take funds away from other necessities in life. Knowing the market as I do, I know there will be plenty of this designer's clothing available on sale or online if I just wait for the right opportunity. A key thought to remember is *there is always more*. There is always more should be a mantra for every Flipster.

Do not let your emotions determine your purchasing. Remember that marketers spend millions of dollars every year on brainwashing advertisements. They want you to believe that you must have certain goods and that you must get them now! Don't be taken in. Instant gratification will cost you.

Getting bargain prices can be as simple as waiting for the end-of-season pricing in the retail store. I purchased a beautiful, classic v-neck cashmere sweater in March for 75 percent off. I will have to delay wearing my new sweater until next fall, but I know winter will return, and I will have a lovely cashmere sweater to start the season. This was a great deal but only because it is a classic style that will not be dated in six months and a high-quality piece that will last for years.

It is better and more frugal to purchase fewer pieces of high-quality, classic clothing than to have a closet full of cheap, low-quality, faddish clothing. Here is another example. Every woman has or should have a pair of black pants. The basic black pant is a wardrobe foundation, and therefore you should buy a nice-quality pair that fits you well and will last for years. Conversely, the summer flip-flop shoe you wear to the beach every year will not stand the test of time. Get that at a bargain basement store, and toss it out at the end of summer. Think about your purchases in advance so you do not make impulse decisions at the store.

Children's clothing is another item that you can buy smartly. Early one year, I purchased a huge lot of Lilly Pulitzer (designer) summer clothing on eBay for our six-year-old daughter. I applied four key principles of smart buying. First, I avoided competition. The auction was in early spring, so most people had just begun to think about summer clothing, and therefore I had little competition in the auction. Secondly, the auction was for twenty pieces of clothing, which sold for just under $200. Most people on eBay feel more comfortable bidding in less expensive auctions with only one or two items, especially when it comes to clothing. Third, I purchased only designer or name brand clothing, because I know that I can resell name-brand clothing at a higher rate of return.

That same summer, I also purchased about thirty pieces of name-brand casual shorts and shirts from a woman at a yard sale for $30—$1 for each piece. So I purchased my daughter's entire summer wardrobe for $230. The following summer I resold all the pieces in smaller auctions, and I actually made money on the transactions. Not only did I dress my daughter in designer clothing that summer for free, I made money in the process.

Finally, I took very good care of her clothing. I think this is a point that must be emphasized, and it applies to anything that you will purchase. Take care of the goods that you purchase. It is frugal and smart to invest in quality items but only if you plan to care for them properly. If you do not know how to care for a particular item, then educate yourself. There are hundreds of websites that will give you instructions on how to clean everything, including fabric, furniture, pottery, vintage jewelry, and more. It makes no sense to buy a designer silk blouse if you wash it with jeans and toss it in the dryer. You will certainly not be able to resell it when it no longer fits your needs.

The power of vision is another fundamental principle that is evident in all the examples. You must be able to think about your purchases as long- or short-term investments. Think of your purchases as money that you are going to invest. Be conscious of your spending and what you hope to gain from every purchase. It does not matter if it is an appliance, a work of art, or a piece of clothing; think about the resale value or ultimate disposal of the item. Many people work very hard to invest their extra money in stocks or retirement plans, but they throw away thousands of dollars every year by inadequate purchasing. You should spend as much time on your current purchasing decisions as you do on you future investment plans. Both are equally important for a strong financial future. We will discuss more on investment purchasing in later chapters.

1 *WordNet® 2.1*. Princeton University. 19 Mar. 2007.
<Dictionary.com http://dictionary.reference.com/browse/frugal>.

Chapter Two
L is for Luxury

Luxury n **1**: Something inessential but conducive to pleasure and comfort **2**: Sumptuous living or surroundings (lives in luxury)[1]

LIVING IN LUXURY MADE SIMPLE

I like going to spas. While I am dubious of the actual health benefits, I find it relaxing and pleasurable, so I treat myself to a spa trip once or twice a year. As a rule, spa prices are not up for negotiation, and they can be quite expensive. So how does a frugal person justify spending a carefree day at the spa? The answer is by being frugal in other areas of daily life.

Let's take sunglasses for example. I believe that it is important to protect my eyes from the sun, so I want to have good-quality sunglasses that offer protection. However, I tend to misplace, break, or loose my sunglasses, so I do not want to invest a great deal of money in them. Just this past summer, while riding the waves at Hilton Head with my daughter, a big wave crashed down upon us, and my sunglasses were lost at sea. Somewhere off the coast of South Carolina, a very nice pair of Ray-Bans is floating around. I would have been upset if I had paid retail for those Ray-Bans. I have acquired at least five pairs of Ray-Bans, but I have not purchased a pair of sunglasses at a retail store for at least six years. Daren has purchased each pair for a dollar or two at yard sales.

Sunglasses styles change quickly, and people like to get a new pair every year, so they discard the old ones even though they are in very good to excellent condition. It really does not matter to me if I have the latest sunglass fashion. I just want glasses that they are functional and look decent on me. So instead of spending $100 or more every year for sunglasses, I use that money toward daily expenses or a trip to the spa. A $100-expenditure may not seem important when looking at total expenses for the year, but every purchase adds up.

Also, when my stash of sunglasses becomes more numerous than I think I will need, I sell the excess pairs on eBay and make money. So not only am I saving money by not buying expensive sunglasses every year, I am making money by reselling designer sunglasses that I do not need. Over the years, we have sold many name-brand sunglasses on eBay at a very nice profit. When looking for used sunglasses, make sure that they are not scratched or damaged.

The key here is to think about what is important to you and how much money you are willing to allocate to a given luxury or necessity. Think about this for both the big and small purchases in your life. Look at the expenses in your life that have become routine, and ask yourself if those expenses are really worth the money you are investing in them. I know of several people who believe that they must stop every morning for an expensive cup of coffee. They spend over three dollars a day on the coffee. If you do the math, you will see that, at five days a week for fifty-two weeks, these daily coffee buyers spend over $780 a year on their coffee consumption. Dropping three dollars a day may not seem like much, but when you look at it as a yearly expense, you quickly realize that it has become an expensive habit.

In the past, there has been a stigma about going to yard sales or flea markets to purchase second-hand goods, but I believe that is beginning to change. Consumers have never had a problem purchasing expensive items such as cars, boats, or homes secondhand, but now people are beginning to see the benefit of previously owned goods for other luxury-type items. Short-term ownership of certain goods is becoming a new way of life, popular even in the upper-income households. For example, you can now lease designer handbags at www.bagborroworsteal.com. Three years ago, no one would have ever thought Prada, Chanel, or Gucci would be available for rent. It actually makes good sense to lease an expensive purse you will only carry for a short time or for a special occasion.

Famous auctions houses such as Sotheby's, Christies, and Doyle's have been selling secondhand merchandise to the wealthy for over two hundred years. While in the past, auction houses were strictly for society's elite, in today's market, all levels of auctions can be found in every state. In the past, live auctions were just about the only place to find quality secondhand goods; now there are more choices. For example, eBay is the fastest-growing secondary market in the world. Consignment shops, pawn shop, yard sales, and flea markets have a steady supply of merchandise. See our chapter on sourcing for more details on where to find quality and luxury items.

When we speak of buying luxury items to resell or for personal use, we are speaking about luxury items of all levels. For a person making minimum wage, a

$100 Citizen watch would be a luxury item. To a person who is making a million dollars a year, a Citizen watch is not a luxury item, but a $30,000 Jaeger-LeCoultre watch would be. Most of us will fall somewhere in the middle of these two extremes. The point we are trying to make is that everyone, no matter what his or her income, has certain items that are just out of economic reach. So when you go out to purchase items specifically to resell or for your own use, keep the resale value in mind.

There are all levels of potential buyers seeking merchandise and all levels of merchandise being sold. The men's line of the Ralph Lauren Company sells different levels of merchandise: Ralph Lauren Chaps, Polo, and Ralph Lauren Purple Label. The Chaps brand carries the lowest-cost items aimed at the good but low-end market. Polo is for the mid-market, and the Purple Label is their highest-quality merchandise. The Ralph Lauren Company also has other labels such as Lauren by Ralph Lauren and Ralph Lauren Home that are geared to particular markets. Ralph Lauren is only one example of many companies that use this marketing technique to sell to the widest possible marketplace. Keep in mind that, not only are there different levels of goods from brand name to brand name, but sometimes *within* a brand name.

The key is to know which level your items fall into before you make a purchase. Some name-brand items have a higher resale value than others due to quality of the item or name recognition of the brand or other factors. In the first appendix, we will provide you with a good, better, best list of some of the most popular brand names and items for the resale market. If you prefer to buy items for short-term use, then you should purchase quality items that will hold their value in the resale market.

1) The American Heritage® Dictionary of the English Language, Fourth Edition. Retrieved March 19, 2007, from Dictionary.com website: http://dictionary.reference.com/browse/luxury

Chapter Three
I is for Investment

Investment n 1:Property or another possession acquired for future financial return or benefit.[1] 2: A commitment, as of time or support.[2]

INVEST WISELY IN YOUR ASSETS WITH AN EYE ON TOMORROW'S MARKETPLACE

We included two definitions for the word investment, and we will cover both in this chapter. The first definition covers the actual assets you will purchase, and the second encompasses the time you will invest in the purchase of such assets.

Not every item that you purchase should be considered an investment purchase. Everyday items such as food, gas, and utilities are considered consumables and are usually nonnegotiable. It is the other items that we will be discussing here. The Flipster System will enable you to increase your buying power on those items and thus be able to afford the nonnegotiable items that are required or that you desire.

When it comes time to purchase an investment asset, you will need to decide if you want to purchase the item new or used. This will always be a personal decision based on what is important to you and the funds you have available for this item. For example, there are many people who like the latest stereo equipment, and that asset is very important to them. Those people are willing to pay top dollar to get the latest and greatest sound system. If you fall into that category, then you should decide what features you are looking for and investigate what brands are available that fit your needs. Then you should look at the resale value of those brands to determine which will offer you the most return on your sound system investment. Since you place a high value on the latest stereo equipment, it is likely you will be replacing your equipment on a regular basis, so this purchase should be treated as a temporary asset. Therefore, if you are considering two brands, and brand A retains 60 percent of its retail price after two years while brand B only retains 40 percent of its retail value, then obviously you should choose to purchase brand A. When you choose to resell the stereo equipment via online auction or another avenue, you can use the money you make reselling this asset to fund, in whole or part, your new asset.

A better way to use the Flipster System is to buy a secondhand, two-year-old stereo at 60 percent of retail cost and use the 40 percent savings to fund your nonnegotiable purchases. The best way to obtain a high-end stereo system is to trade up your purchases. Daren has been upgrading our stereo systems by purchasing from yard sales. What we have found is that yards sales are great places to buy products but not to sell them. If you have anything of value, you do not want to try to sell it at a yard sale. We will discuss this topic in more detail in our chapter on sourcing.

We had a sound system that was acceptable, but it did not have the latest features. So when Daren found one at a yard sale that was better and newer, we sold our old one on eBay. Then several months later Daren got a fantastic deal on a high-end model, so we again sold the older model on eBay and kept the high-end model. The key here is that, not only did we upgrade our stereo system, we made money on the transactions. By making a bargain investment at a yard sale and selling at a more competitive marketplace like eBay, we were able to turn a profit. We then used that profit to finance future purchases. We now have a very nice high-end stereo system, but it took a while to get the system we wanted. If you are willing to wait and trade up as the opportunities come, then you will achieve one of the key factors in the Flipster System. Instant gratification will cost you. Stereo equipment is only one example of how to use this philosophy. The same techniques and philosophy can apply to just about every traditional asset.

The Gown with No Name

A close friend of mine purchased a stunning evening gown to wear to a charity fund-raiser. The dress was lovely, high-quality, elegant, and everything that anyone would want in an evening dress except it did not have a designer label. She had purchased the dress at a very high-end boutique, and the dress carried the label of the boutique. My friend paid $1,200 for the dress, and she tried to sell the dress online to recoup some of the money she had spent. After repeated attempts to sell the dress and lowering her starting price several times, she contacted me.

She asked me to look at her eBay listing to see if I could determine why her dress was not selling. Her listing was fantastic and included several very nice pictures. The problem was not with the listing and not with the dress. The problem was with the label on the inside on the dress. No one outside of her home town of Chicago would recognize the name of the fashionable boutique, so buyers were uneasy about spending a great deal of money on the dress. The listing stated that the dress was well made and from a very nice store, but how could buyers really see that in a picture?

Also, evening gowns are hard to purchase online. Gowns can be cut in a way that is unflattering to certain figures so most women want to try on a gown before purchasing. Buying a sweater online is a little easier than buying evening attire.

I suggested to my friend that she should take her dress to a retail consignment store in the Chicago area. Potential buyers would more likely be familiar with the boutique, and they would be able to try it on before they made their purchase. She stated that she had considered that option but that the consignment store would take 40 percent of the sale price so she was hoping to sell it on eBay. So, I suggested that, the next time she purchases an expensive item, she buy a well-known brand name or designer. That way she will be able to resell the item online.

THE TRADING UP PHILOSOPHY

We have used the trading up philosophy to get better, higher-quality assets for years. When we purchase an asset, we buy with the knowledge that someday in the future we will resell this asset. We sell the old asset to help finance the purchase of the new asset. If you can get a great deal on the original asset purchase, sometimes you can use that asset for years and still turn a profit at resale.

Upgrading Sterling Flatware

When I decided to have the family Thanksgiving dinner at my home, I wanted to have a nice set of sterling silver flatware. But even on eBay, a full set of sterling silver was expensive. So I was very excited when I found a very nice set of Lunt Modern Victorian for only $350 at a local pawn shop. The pieces were in good condition, and there was a full service for eight with some serving pieces. I liked the set and used it for about a year, until I came across a set of Gorham Strasbourg at a tag sale. This set had more serving pieces and was a nicer, heavier set. I purchased it for $675. I broke up the set of Lunt into small auctions and sold it on eBay for a total of just over $600—almost enough to pay for my new set of Gorham.

I had been using the set of Gorham for a little over two years when I came across a great deal on eBay for a service for twelve of Gorham King Edward.

This service had many serving pieces and a two-tiered case, and the flatware was made of heavy antique sterling. The seller had listed the sterling set with a Buy-it-Now price of $1000, so I purchased it quickly.

We will discuss the Buy-it-Now feature later in this book, but for the most part, I do not think it is good for the seller. The feature is great for the buyer, but it could cost the seller a lot of money. Sometimes sellers want to make a quick sale; sometimes they have a price they want to receive, and that is all they are interested in getting for the item.

This story demonstrates how impatience will cost you money. If the seller of the Gorham King Edward set had let the set of flatware go through the auction process, I know that the set would have sold for well over $3,000. At first, I was concerned that this set may not be the quality set that was advertised in the listing. I thought that, since the price was so low, there must be a problem with the set such as damage. I read the listing carefully and paid with the PayPal service so, if there was a problem, I would have recourse.

As luck would have it, I absolutely love this set of sterling. I have been using it for several years, and I doubt I will trade it in—unless I come across a great deal on a Tiffany or Georg Jensen sterling flatware set.

I again broke up my old set. I sold the Strasbourg sterling pieces on eBay for a total of $850. So if you add up everything I spent and everything I made from the buying and selling of my sterling silver flatware, you will find that, in net terms, I only paid $575 for my current set of flatware, and its value is well over $3,000. I also was able to use the other sets of flatware for over three years.

I used the sets of flatware as investment pieces. I purchased the sets knowing that I would want to eventually trade up to better sets of sterling. I was able to achieve my goal of owning a set of Gorham King Edward by trading up my purchases and by smart buying and selling.

Another great tip to keep in mind where flatware is concerned is that on eBay there are more people looking to add to their current flatware than there are people looking to buy a complete set. When I sell flatware sets, I split them up into smaller auctions so there will be more competition in the auctions.

Here's a great tip to remember when buying for resale or for personal use: try to buy in the off-season and sell during the in-season. For example, the price of sterling silver flatware goes up in the late fall just before Thanksgiving and Christmas. So I purchased my Gorham King Edward sterling in the early summer (the off-season) and sold my old Strasbourg sterling in early November (the in-season). Following the same principle, you would not want to sell your Christmas ornaments in July or an Easter dress in November.)

Some items do not have a season and will sell well during any time of the year, but we have found almost everything will do its best during the Christmas season.

As for any retail trade, the Christmas season is the busiest time of the year for reselling. As a matter of fact, we hold back many of our better goods to sell from late October to early December.

Daren and I use this trading up philosophy on just about all our hard assets. We have traded up on artwork, pottery, electronics, china, and even furniture.

We should note at this point that there are some items you would not want to purchase secondhand. These include items that cannot be completely washed or cleaned, such as upholstered furniture and mattresses.

The second definition of the term investment has to do with the investment of your time. Most of you who are reading this book will have regular, full-time jobs that are not in the eBay- or resale-related fields. You will be using the Flipster System for your personal wealth and growth or as a part-time business and hobby. Daren and I have an eBay business, so we can obviously dedicate more of our time to pursue the bargains we have mentioned. We find bargains for ourselves while in the course of business—finding bargains for resale.

In our sourcing chapters, we will provide you with many places where you can go to find great deals on new and used items. You need to decide how much time and effort you are willing to put into your pursuits and determine what level of reselling will be cost effective for you.

While we have certainly found it financially beneficial to get up on Saturday morning to explore the local yard sales for bargains, you may prefer to invest your time at the flea markets, auction houses, or searching for online deals. Also, when it comes time to upgrade and resell your temporary assets, you may want to find an eBay drop-off store or trading assistant to sell your items instead of trying to sell the items yourself.

There are several reasons you may want to do this. Time is one key reason. I have several antique dealers who are my regular customers. They would rather spend their time acquiring the goods to resell then trying to sell them online. I have another regular customer who has a full time job but buys to resell on the side. Both these types of customers know that their limited time is better used in acquiring the goods for resale or earning a paycheck. They leave the online selling up to someone else.

Also, selling effectively on eBay is more difficult than buying on eBay. You have to have the equipment to take a very good picture, know the proper key words to draw people to your auctions, and pack and ship the items. Selling online can be a very time-consuming activity, especially when you are not set up to sell on a regular basis.

Another factor to consider is, until you become established on eBay and have a lot of positive feedback, some buyers may consider it risky to buy from you. Few buyers are willing to purchase expensive goods from a new seller. This is why using an established trading assistant or drop-off store could be beneficial.

Of course you also need to be very cautious when choosing a drop-off store to handle your goods. Many of the new franchises that are coming into the marketplace are owned and staffed by people with little to no experience. Some of these franchises make a good deal of their profits by charging huge shipping fees to buyers. When buyers decide to bid on an item and see an exorbitant shipping charge, they will factor that into their ultimate bid or not bid at all. This means less money for you. The practice is so prevalent in fact that the Bill Cobb, President of eBay North American, sent an email in July 2006 addressing the eBay community with his concerns about the problem. He stated that the number one reason potential buyers leave eBay is due to excessive shipping and handling charges. He then assured eBay shoppers that the site will aggressively fight sellers who add excessive fees to their shipping charges.

If you are selling antiques or collectibles through a trading assistant or drop-off store, make sure you go over the key words the assistant may want to use to sell your item. A proper title is extremely important when selling on eBay. If your listing is missing key search words, buyers will not be able to find your listing. I would also recommend testing the assistant with a few items before giving him or her a large number of expensive items to sell. Make sure that he or she lists the items and pays you in a timely manner.

When our business, eBizAuctions, sells on consignment, we offer more to our customers than taking a picture of their item and listing it on eBay. Selling on consignment means selling items for others for a percentage of the sale price. Many times we have to research the item to make sure that we are listing it properly. We have hundreds of books that we use as guides, we perform online research, and we have a pool of experts in specific areas that we can count on for opinions. Daren is a Certified and Licensed Auctioneer and I am a Certified Personal Property Appraiser. If you believe you have antiques or collectibles that are of high value, we would recommend finding a seller who has some experience with these items.

1) *The American Heritage® Dictionary of the English Language, Fourth Edition.* Retrieved March 19, 2007, from Dictionary.com website: http://dictionary.reference.com/browse/Investment

2) *The American Heritage® Dictionary of the English Language, Fourth Edition.* Retrieved March 19, 2007, from Dictionary.com website: http://dictionary.reference.com/browse/Investment

Chapter Four
P is for Purchasing

Purchasing v: To acquire by effort; earn.[1]

PURCHASING SHOULD REQUIRE EFFORT AND NOT BE AN AUTOMATIC FUNCTION

I like the definition of purchasing as written above. I think too many people go through life automatically purchasing items without thinking about what they are spending and what alternatives they have available to them.

If you are purchasing just to acquire better assets for yourself, then your needs and desires will play the lead role in what you purchase. However, if you want to use the Flipster System to not only obtain better quality goods for yourself but also to make extra income by buying to resell, then price should be your major focus.

THE eBay EFFECT

Any market analyst will tell you that eBay has had an effect on just about every conceivable consumer good, and the site has only been in operation for twelve years. Millions of people are regular eBay shoppers now, and there will be millions more in the future as we speed forward on this fast-paced technology superhighway. While many markets have just begun to feel this eBay effect, the antiques and collectibles markets have already been greatly affected. This may be because, when eBay started, it was mainly used as a forum to sell collectibles. Whatever the reason, eBay has completely changed the demand and availability of antiques and collectibles. Before eBay and other online auctions, collectors would have to search months or years to find a new piece for their collection. They would go from city to town and from antique stores to flea markets in search of that elusive, rare piece to enhance their collection. The thrill of the hunt has now been replaced by the click of the mouse. Twenty four hours a day, seven days a week, any person with a computer can log onto eBay and search. This has made the market switch from a seller's market to a buyer's market, which has, for the most part, caused prices to go down. Many antique stores have closed their doors, because they cannot compete with the online market. Others have joined the online marketplace.

Daren and I visited a local antique store and saw a McCoy planter with a price of $55. This was a typical figural McCoy planter in very good condition. Later in the evening, we ran a search on eBay for that specific planter. In the previous two months, the same planter had sold twenty-eight times for an average of $22. So even with the added expense of shipping, buying online can save the buyer a great deal of money. The auction site eBay has lowered the price of almost every collectible on the market, and the average antique store cannot compete.

One afternoon in July 2006, I ran a search for the following popular collectibles. I think most people would be shocked to know how many popular collectibles and art objects are available on eBay at any given moment. Keep in mind these were current auctions, not a history of auctions that had been open in months past. Here are some of the search words I plugged into the site's search engine and the numbers those searches generated:

Item	Number of open auctions on eBay
Barbie:	2,810
Roseville:	1,580
Disney:	111,329
McCoy:	3,919
Hot Wheels:	14,101
Waterford:	2,914

You can find similar results by simply plugging in just about any antique or collectible as a search word on the site.

In years past, a certain collectible may have been plentiful in the Ohio area but very hard to find in the northeast. Collectors in the northeast would have paid a premium price to obtain that collectible. So eBay has leveled the playing field. Geographic location is no longer an obstacle to purchasing. Even sellers located in other countries can tap into the American market with shipping costs being their only limitation, and American sellers likewise can open up their auctions to international buyers.

Jack Daniels in London

> We had purchased a vintage Jack Daniels collectible bottle and listed it on eBay. The high bidder was a gentleman in London, England. The bottle was very heavy and expensive to ship, but he was willing to pay the price of shipping, because Jack Daniels bottles were made in the United States and thus are extremely scarce in Great Britain.

Another important point to factor into your purchasing decision is that there will always be people who will be willing to "take whatever they can get" for an item. I have had many customers come to me asking me to liquidate an estate that they have inherited. Those items have no special meaning to them, and they did not invest their own money into the purchase of those assets. Many times they have no idea of the value and see the items as more of a burden than a potential cash machine. They may know or think that the goods have some value, but the quick disposal of the goods is more important than the monetary gain. These goods may have come to them at an emotional time. They may have no way to store or transport the goods, and they may not have the time, energy, or knowledge to seek out the best, most profitable disposal of the assets.

I have had customers who have brought me merchandise from their retail stores that have gone out of business. These customers must liquidate their inventory because they have terminated their leases and must move any remaining merchandise out of the retail space. Generating any profit from the sale of these goods is better than dumping them in the trash.

But my biggest group of customers is people who are downsizing. They are moving to smaller homes, they just do not have the room to take all their belongings with them, and they are desperate to recoup some of the investment that they have in these items.

All these types of customers just want to get some money out of their assets. These customers usually tell me to start the bidding at a low opening bid and let the market set the price. While this may seem discouraging to someone who wants to buy to resell, fear not; eBay is large enough now that sellers can get a decent, fair market value on most goods, and those goods that are truly rare and/or expensive will yield fantastic returns.

We have covered the antiques and collectibles markets, but there is a huge market for everyday items such as clothing, shoes, cookware, jewelry, and other household items as well. There are many sellers on eBay and other online auctions who make their primary or secondary income by purchasing at factory outlets, wholesalers, and closeouts. They buy new, name-brand goods at deep discounts and resell online. This can be a great way to make income if you can find a steady source of product. However, clothing styles, technology trends, and popularity can change rapidly, so you must keep current and know the prices that the market will bear.

There is also a great market for moderately-used items, especially those that have a recognizable name brand. When you are purchasing items, keep in mind that high-quality name-brand and designer goods will always sell better than no-name or discount store-brand items. When purchasing, keep the original retail price in mind, knowing that you will only get a fraction of that original cost at auction. This is a general rule that mainly applies to current retail items (or items that were on the retail shelf in the very recent past.) There are always exceptions to the rules. A hot toy, a designer handbag in limited production, or a new electronic gadget can exceed its current retail price if it is hard to find and in limited supply. Sometimes a vintage piece from a designer collection will receive three or four times the original cost. It just depends on the condition, the designer, and the product itself.

There are several reasons why name-brand items sell better online. The first is that when buying online a buyer must search by auction title. There is no store to browse, so a cute little bobble will not catch the eye. The buyer must actively search for items by name. Secondly, when buyers purchase a Liz Claiborne jacket or a Le Creuset stock pot, they know exactly what they will receive. A seller can write a beautiful description telling potential buyers how wonderful an item is, but if that brand is unknown to the buyer, he or she will likely pay less or pass it up.

BUY LOW; SELL HIGH

Although it seems like a pretty simple concept, buying low and selling high is much harder to put into action. This is why we recommend that you start out by reselling things that you are familiar with and have researched. We know of a woman who was an expert on designer jeans. She took this knowledge and started reselling designer jeans that she'd purchased at thrift shops. Her confidence increased with every moneymaking sale, and she gained knowledge in other designer clothing areas and thus was able to expand the items she offered. She also began to search other sources for more products, such as consignment shops and yard sales. As she learned her market, she was able to purchase more expensive designer label goods and expanded into other designer clothing, thus increase her profits. She knew which designers were hot and which products retained a higher resale value in the secondary marketplace. This is a great example of how someone can use his or her current knowledge base to make money in the online market. What is your knowledge base? How can you use that knowledge to find and resale items online?

No matter what area you choose to start your resale endeavor in, you should continually seek to broaden your knowledge base and stay current on prices.

LEARN FROM YOUR MISTAKES

We will discuss these concepts in greater depth in later chapters, but I want to mention here that there will be bad purchases along the way. Especially when you are learning and adjusting to the online price fluctuations, you will eventually make a purchase that is not profitable. But do not let a few mistakes discourage you. Don't let the fear of a bad purchase paralyze you into missing the smart-risk purchases. Daren and I have made a great deal of profit from gut-feelings purchases. Do not be foolish; wait until you have had some practice before you start to rely on gut feelings. Also, make sure you learn from your mistake when you make one. Find out why the item did not sell as you thought it should. Did it have a recognizable brand name? Was the condition poor? Did you buy it because you liked it and thought everyone else would like it too?

The Silver that Caught My Eye

I purchased a silver chafing dish at an estate sale, because I love silver items and thought it was a lovely piece. I paid too much money for the dish. I knew in my gut that it was not going to be a good seller, but I talked myself into purchasing the dish because it was so pretty. At first glance, a lovely silver-plated chafing dish would seem like a great thing to purchase for resale. It was in great condition and had ornate scroll feet and a lion's head on the front. What I failed to take into consideration is that most people do not entertain with this type of cookware anymore. People are more inclined to have simple, casual meals and are not in the market for a silver chafing dish.

1) *Dictionary.com Unabridged (v 1.1)*. Retrieved March 19, 2007, from Dictionary.com website: http://dictionary.reference.com/browse/Purchasing

Chapter Five
Getting Started

Some of you will simply want to resell your luxury goods in order to finance more, newer, and better goods. Others will want to start reselling on a part- or full-time basis in order to make a profit. Either way, before getting started, you will first have to decide whether to sell for yourself or have a trading assistant sell for you. In this chapter, we will give you pointers on how to make that decision. For those who want to work with a trading assistant, we'll give you guidance on choosing a good one. And, for those do-it-yourselfers, we'll cover basic strategies for selling on eBay. In chapter six, we'll cover selling for a profit in more detail.

The eBay website is a very good place to resell items, and every reseller should be familiar with this online auction service. The great thing about eBay and other online auctions is that they allow anyone with a computer easy access to millions of shoppers. There are other great places to sell goods, and they will all be discussed in the sourcing chapter.

CHOOSING WHETHER OR NOT TO SELL FOR YOURSELF

The first thing you must decide before you begin to resell your own goods is whether you want to do it yourself or have a trading assistant sell for you. Ask yourself how much free time you have. Selling on eBay takes more time than you may expect. If you work a full-time job and have children or time-consuming activities or hobbies, then you may want to consider a trading assistant. Also, ask yourself how valuable your time is to you. If you make more than $40,000 a year or highly value your free time, then a trading assistant may be the choice for you. However, if lack of time is not a problem for you or if you think selling online would be a great hobby, then you may want sell items for yourself. A trading assistant usually takes between 30 to 40 percent of the final sale price, so you must decide whether your time or the extra money is more important to you. Also, if you are the type of person who is not self-motivated, then you may want to consider a trading assistant. If you know your items are going to sit unsold for months, then it may be to your benefit to hire the job out.

FINDING A TRADING ASSISTANT

If you decide you would prefer to have someone else sell your items, you will need to find the right person. You can find a list on eBay of trading assistants who sell all over the country, and you can find drop-off store locations in your local telephone book. Take the time to interview the trading assistant, because this is someone who will put money in your pocket. An inexperienced trading assistant can cost you hundred or thousands of dollars.

Some important questions to ask a potential trading assistant include:

- How long have you been a trading assistant?
- Do you sell on eBay on a full- or part-time basis?
- What are your fees?
- How long will it take for my items to appear on eBay?
- When can I expect payment?
- Who sets the starting price for my items?
- What are your selling qualifications or experience?
- Do you have references?

Get the trading assistants' eBay user ID and look at their feedback and how long they have been registered users on eBay. I do not have perfect feedback and would not expect anyone else to have perfect feedback; there will always be buyers that are unreasonable and cannot be pleased. But a good trading assistant should have at least a 99 percent positive rating. Look at potential trading assistants' current and past auctions. Are the pictures professional and the descriptions clear? Do the listings have long lists of harsh and unreasonable rules? That is usually a turnoff to buyers. Are their shipping fees reasonable? Shipping is very expensive, and handling fees are normal as long as they are not excessive. Ask yourself if you would feel comfortable buying from this seller. Always test the trading assistant with a small number of items before giving him or her all your items or your very expensive items.

Our company, eBizAuctions, rarely, if ever advertises. Over 90 percent of our business is from repeat or referred customers. We always have enough or more business than we can handle. We could expand and hire more employees, but I like the way we operate. I like my small business and the freedom that it affords me. I want to be in the antiques business not in the business of being in business.

SELLING ONLINE FOR YOURSELF

For the purposes of this chapter, our main focus will be selling your items at an online auction. *However, the online marketplace is not the only or necessarily the best place to sell your goods.* There is a great deal of merchandise that would be better sold at other venues. If you have furniture, rare antiques, or highly specialized items, you may want to consider traditional auctions, tag sales, or selling directly to an antique dealer. We are big proponents of the auction method, both traditional and online. The online marketplace has an undefined ceiling on the price that buyers are willing to pay for goods that they cannot inspect in person. However, if the auction is properly conducted, that format will *almost always* earn you fair market value.

Selling your goods via tag sales or directly to a dealer has some inherent problems. If you sell directly to a dealer, they will want to pay you as little as possible, because they are going to have to resell the goods. If you have ever driven by a tag sale, you will see long lines of people waiting out front to get in. Why is this? It has been our experience that, for the most part, the people running these sales do not have the broad-range knowledge to price items at their fair market value. So bargain hunters line up for the chance to get great deals. Some items are priced very inexpensively, and others are priced too high. Please see our section on sourcing to find out more details on places to buy and sell your goods.

If you decide that you want to sell your own items, then you need to make some small investments. You will need access to a computer, a digital camera, at least two backdrops (one dark and one light), boxes, and packing material. You will also need to have a seller's ID on eBay or your choice of other online auctions. If you do not have an eBay ID, put this book down and go sign up right now. If you did not have an eBay user ID or you have only been a user for a short period of time, you may want to consider a trading assistant until you have some time and feedback under your ID. The best and quickest way to get some positive feedback is to buy items on eBay. Buyers will be leery of a new seller or one with just a few feedbacks. You will also need a basic understanding of how to sell on eBay. An in-depth discussion on how to correctly sell on eBay is not the purpose of this book, but we recommend that you educate yourself on this topic.

You will also have to decide on which methods of payments you will accept. Only accepting money orders will limit your customers. You will need to sign up with an online payment service such as PayPal. Paypal's website is located at https://www.paypal.com. Again, you will need to familiarize yourself with that service and the company's rules. I highly recommend that you read all the rules and information regarding the fees. For example, if you do not have online tracking or delivery confirmation on all your packages, buyers could state that they never received the package and have their money returned to them from your PayPal account. Be sure to read PayPal's seller's protection policy before you begin selling on eBay.

SHIPPING DECISIONS

You will also need to make a decision on how you will ship your items. The United States Postal Office provides free priority mail boxes, which helps to keep costs down. But unless everything that you plan to sell will fit in a twelve-inch square or smaller box, you will need more options. You can print your postage online with a credit card, and your postal carrier will pick up the packages at your home for free.

For larger boxes, the three main carriers are Federal Express, UPS, and DHL. All three offer online shipping and free tracking. I have tried all three carriers, and I have decided to go with Federal Express for a number of reasons. They have consistent on-time delivery, their prices are fair, their billing is accurate, and my sales representative has always offered me excellent service. If you ship more than ten packages a week, you should negotiate the cost of your shipping fees with the carrier. If you only plan to ship a few package every month, you should find a local drop-off site to take your packages instead of paying for a pickup at your home.

One tip I want to mention here is that *it is always better to over-pack than under-pack an item.* If an item gets broken during shipment, you will have to refund the cost of the item and/or file a claim with the shipper. No matter what carrier you use—and I have used them all—the companies make it extremely difficult to file a claim and get paid. I am sure that they do this to discourage frivolous claims, but it is such a headache and so time-consuming that, on some small claims, I just pay the money out of my pocket to avoid all the lost time I would spend trying to get the carrier to pay a claim. Another option is to have the buyer file the claim with the carrier. You will still have to provide some information, but the majority of the headache will be transferred to the buyer. Make sure you note that claims will be the buyer's responsibility upfront. State clearly that the buyer is responsible for filing any lost or damaged claims but that you will cooperate by providing any needed documentation.

The point here is that you should pack very well, using a strong box and plenty of packing material. Also know that most carriers will not cover antiques and collectibles, even if you purchase the extra insurance. Note that the carriers use the term *declared value* rather than insurance. All the major carriers except the United States Postal Service have a clause in their agreements that release them from covering any item that has a value greater than $100, and that value is based on its age or rarity. So be sure to read the fine print in your service agreement and ship accordingly.

WHAT TO SELL FIRST

After you have figured out all of the above, you can finally get down to making some money. If you are like most Americans, you will have closets full of items you have not used in years. You may also have an attic or basement filled with forgotten treasures. Just pick a place and start finding your valuables. Once you have gathered a box or two of items that you want to sell, take the time to research. If you plan to sell the items on eBay, either yourself or through a trading assistant, search the completed auctions on eBay to see how much your items will bring in the open market. We have found that, when all variables are considered, eBay is a fairly consistent marketplace.

When searching on eBay for the market price of your items, be sure to look in the completed listings. Many buyers do not bid until the final seconds of an auction. The true value of the item will not be revealed until the close of the auction. Also consider the variables of age, condition, and style when searching. If your Kate Spade purse is five years old and has a broken strap, expect it sell for much less than a Kate Spade purse that is less than a year old and is in perfect condition sold for. You will need to read the description of the listing to determine if the item you see on eBay is similar to the item you plan on selling.

THE SCIENCE OF SETTING THE PRICE

The next thing you need to determine is the starting price. I am a firm believer in starting an auction low with no reserve. Buyers like low-starting, no-reserve auctions and are much more likely to get in a bidding war when the item starts at a reasonable or low bid. If you start the auction too high, you will discourage bidders and most likely not sell your item. The online auction is similar to a live auction in that it grabs at a person's emotions. Sometimes people will get carried away at a live auction and keep bidding even after they have gone over their preset limit. This happens in the online auction too. You want people to get emotionally involved with the purchase of your item. You want people to believe that that item belongs to them; you want them to see the item you're selling in their homes or envision wearing it.

At a live or online auction, a person will set a mental limit of what they are willing to pay. For example, let us say that I have a Weller Vase up for auction that should sell for anywhere from $300 to $400. A buyer searches and finds my vase starting at a ridiculously low price of $9.99. This buyer is a Weller collector and knows the vase is worth at least $300 dollars, so he believes that he may get a real bargain. He makes a mental limit of what he is willing to spend. He sets his limit at $275. He watches the auction all week long while potential buyers slowly start to place bids. During the week, our imaginary bidder imagines owning the vase and plans where he will display the vase in his home. He becomes emotionally attached to the vase. With just a few hours left, bids have only reached $175.

Then, with just a few minutes left in the auction, all the Weller collectors begin to bid on the vase, and the price climbs to $290. Because the collector is emotionally attached to the vase, he decides to raise his limit to $300. He does not want to lose the vase he has dreamed about all week. With just a few seconds left in the auction, the bidding reaches $310. So the collector once again readjusts his maximum bid. He decides to go just a little higher, up to $340.

This is what you want to happen to all your auction listings. You want people to become emotionally involved in the auction and bid as high as possible. If I had started the bidding at $300, then I would have lost this bidder and, most likely, many others. This bidder would have passed my auction over and not bid at all, because he would have thought the starting price was too high. But because I started the bid low, the collector got emotionally involved in the bidding. He saw the vase as part of his collection even before he began to bid on it himself. I know this happens all the time. I have seen it at live auctions, and I have seen it happen on online auctions. I must confess that, even though I consider myself to be an experienced auction buyer, I have had it happen to me. I usually do this when I am bidding on a cute little outfit for my daughter. I watch the auction all week and envision her in the outfit. So when I am outbid, I will usually go just a little higher.

UNREALISTIC PRICING

The worst thing that you can do in an online auction is to start your auction at an unrealistic price. I see this all the time on eBay, and every time I see it I wonder why the seller did not research the item before he or she listed it at such an outrageously high price. I have seen sellers start an item at four or five times the going rate, and it is just a waste of their time and their money. Every time you list an item on eBay, you must pay a listing fee, even if the item does not sell. The listing fee ranges from thirty cents to $10, so you are throwing away your money if you start an item at an unrealistic price. I have, at times, checked sellers' histories and seen that they have listed the same item over and over again at that same outrageous price. You would think that after the third or fourth no sale, they would realize there is a problem. Keep in mind that they have had to pay a listing fee each time they've re-listed the item, so they've lost money repeatedly on an item that has no chance of selling.

There may be a rare instance when you can list an item at an unrealistic price and it will sell, but I would not make that my plan for a successful business. The market sets the price—it's a fundamental principal of supply and demand that is taught to every first-year economics student. In the beginning, it will take a great deal of guts and courage to start your auctions low or below what you paid for the items you're selling, but if you buy wisely, the risk should be small.

If you are a registered eBay user, you can check the histories of completed sales. This allows you to research what items similar to the ones you plan to sell have recently sold for. You also have access to a market research service, which allows you to search the last three months of eBay history. There is a small monthly fee for this service, but if you are going to sell on eBay, it is worth the cost. I think it is an extremely valuable tool, especially if you are selling on consignment. By using this service, you can give your consignment customer a realistic sales price expectation for items sold on eBay. Be sure to take into consideration variables, such as condition, when using the market research tools. If you consider all the variables, the market research tool is usually a very accurate predictor of future price performance. If you have a truly rare or unusual item, you may find that there is no sales history, and you will have to determine whether you want to risk letting the market set the price.

SOMETIMES YOU HAVE TO CUT YOUR LOSSES

I have a customer who is a delightful man in every aspect except one: pricing his items. Regardless of an item's market price, he will insist on starting the item at more than what he paid for the piece. This customer has a retail store where he sells both new and used goods, but he calls on me from time to time to sell certain items for him on eBay. He has in his store a large collection of cameras and other photographic equipment. I call it a collection because it has become a collection—by accident not intention. My customer has had this collection for as long as I have known him, which is about three years now. Every so often, I will bring up the fact that these cameras are getting more out of date every day and suggest that he unload them as soon as possible. His response is always the same. He says that he has more invested in them than he could ever get out of them. Of course the longer he holds on to these technology-based items, the more they will depreciate until they are worthless.

My advice is and has always been that it is better to get something back for the goods then to get nothing at all. If this customer had sold the items three years ago, he may have lost 30 percent of his investment. If he were to sell them today, he may loose 50 percent. But if he waits another three years, he will likely loose 80 percent. He is also tying up his shelf space with items that are not selling rather than using it to stock more productive (saleable) goods.

The point of this example is that sometimes you have to cut your losses. If you make a poor purchase, it is better to recuperate some of your investment then to hold onto something in a futile hope that you may be able to make a profit in the distant future. While it is perfectly acceptable to wait until the best time to sell an item, you need to be realistic in setting the price. Holding onto your skiing equipment until winter is a smart choice, but holding onto outdated cameras for three years is a waste of your capital.

TO RESERVE OR NOT TO RESERVE

On eBay and most other online auctions, sellers can set reserve amounts on their auctions. A reserve is a set amount—usually hidden from the buyer—that an auction must reach before the item will sell. For example, I could have listed my Weller vase to start at $9.99, but put a reserve of $300 on the piece. Bidders would have had to bid against each other up to the $300 reserve amount, or the piece would have remained unsold.

I am not a fan of the reserve auction. It discourages bidders and keeps an item from selling at fair market value. If I am interested in an auction, and I see it has a reserve, I will pass it by and will not watch or track the auction. I have also found that people put too high a reserve on their items. Again, some simple online research will save you from wasting your money. If the online marketplace will not produce the price you need or want to get for an item, then you should try to sell the piece at another venue. Do not put a high reserve on something and then hope people are foolish. I would rather see an item start at a higher price than see it have a reserve. I prefer this because, if an auction has a reserve, then two or more people must bid against each other in order to reach the reserve so that the item will sell. By contrast, if you have a higher opening bid price and you find one person who is willing to pay that price, then the item will sell.

Over the years, we have put hundreds of items up for auction that have not sold the first time around but, in a second auction where we set a lower starting price, have sold for more than we had originally started the first auction. For the most part, we start all of our own auctions at $9.99. This can be a risky endeavor, but we are confident that we will get the fair market value for a piece.

As I have said, both Daren and I are true believers in the auction method, and we believe you should start with a low opening bid with no reserve. However, in the beginning you may prefer to start your item at a slightly higher price so you can feel comfortable with the auction process. If you must have a reserve price, then state the reserve price in the auction. Listing the reserve does not change anything, but it lets potential buyers know whether you are being reasonable and they should take the time to bid or you are being unreasonable with your expectations and they should move to another seller.

LISTING TO SELL

In online auctions, listing items properly is imperative. Listings are the only way potential buyers will find the items you have to sell.

A Picture is Worth a Thousand Words or a Few Hundred Bucks

Take great pictures. Remember potential buyers must rely on your pictures to determine whether they want the item. You do not have to spend a great deal of money to accomplish this task. Invest in a good basic digital camera. Purchase backgrounds so your pictures look professional. I hate to see pictures taken on the dining room table or dirty floors; I lose faith in the seller and fear that I may have problems with the sale if I decide to bid. I came upon some very nice steak knives up for auction on eBay. However, the picture of the knives was taken on the back of a toilet. You could see the dirty toilet and stained wall behind the knives. I do not know how any potential buyer would want these knives after seeing this picture. Go to the fabric store and get some sturdy fabric as a backdrop. I recommend vinyl so you can wipe it clean. You can use a staple gun to attach the fabric to a large wooden dowel so you can roll it up for easy storage. You will also need lighting. Until you get up and running and have made some money, you can make do with lighting from lamps or lighting purchased at home-improvement stores. When it comes time to reinvest in your business, you can purchase some professional lighting.

Writing a Description

Write a complete but brief description. In your description you want to give all the important facts about an item such as size, condition, age, and maker or brand. If a buyer needs more information on an item, he or she can email you a question. Try to include all the information about an item so that every question a buyer may have is already covered in the description. You want to limit the questions a buyer will need to ask, because it is time-consuming for you to answer questions, and when all the information is not presented upfront, buyers may be discouraged from bidding. In your description, it is not necessary to go into great detail describing the piece. You should take great pictures so potential buyers can see for themselves that the piece is a fan-shaped vase with two handles.

Also, do not go on with boring details that are of no relevance to the item up for sale. I have seen people write descriptions on how they used the item in their Florida home, but now they are downsizing and must sell some of their possessions. First, unneeded and unrelated information can distract the buyer from bidding on the item. Second, airing personal information in an auction listing is unprofessional, and you never know when something you say will turn off a potential bidder. Third, when you have too much unnecessary information crammed into a listing, the important points about the item can get lost. You do not want potential bidders to abandon your listing because they had to filter through three hundred words about your recent gallbladder surgery just to learn the size of the bowl up for auction. But most importantly, you should value your time more. I have seen people write a thousand words in a single auction listing, most of which have nothing to do with the item up for sale. The average description should be no more than fifty words. If you have a group of items in one auction, the word count can be greater, but remember the old saying by Thomas Jefferson: "The most valuable of all talents is never using two words when one will do."

KEEP YOUR ACCOUNTS ORGANIZED

I have found that the easiest way to stay organized while selling many items online is to keep everything on a week-to-week schedule. I start all my auctions on Saturday or Sunday, because I believe that is the best time to sell my items on eBay. I run all my auctions for seven days, which means that all my auctions will end on a Saturday or Sunday. I list during the week, but I use the scheduling feature so that the auction starts on Saturday. Using this system compartmentalizes items into weeks, which makes it much easier to keep track of shipping and non-paying bidders. If you have consignment customers, it also makes it easier to record and keep track of payments that need to be made to them. I try to list all the items of one consignment customer in one week. Sometimes customers will have too many items, so I have to sell their items over a two- or three-week period. However, the vast majority of customers will have less than fifteen items, so listing their entire collection is not usually a problem. Once a customer's items sell and I have received payment, I can cut him or her one check for the entire amount.

If you start your auctions every day of the week, it will be much harder to notice if a bidder has not paid in a timely manner or if an item has not been shipped.

I also set aside Monday morning to perform bookkeeping chores. This is the time I write checks to consignors, pay bills, and perform any other bookkeeping-related tasks. If you sell for others, it is imperative that you keep meticulous records and pay in a timely manner. I would estimate that over 95 percent of my business comes from repeat customers or referrals from past customers, so it is important to provide good service.

DEALING WITH DAMAGE

One final tip I would like to share is to always list any imperfections the piece may have. It is tempting to gloss over any minor damage or fault in a piece, but that would be a mistake. Most buyers will carefully examine items they receive and ask for a reduction in the price or to return the item for a refund if they find a problem that was not mentioned. Shipping is a major expense when selling online, and you do not want to absorb the cost of a return.

Dealing with an unhappy customer also takes time. The few extra dollars that may be bid because you presented an item as being in a better condition than it is will not outweigh the time and money you'll have to spend on returns.

Some sellers will offer a discount for an item that has damage not mentioned in the listing. I have made it a policy not to offer reductions for any reason. I have made a few exceptions over the years, but very few. I made this policy in 2004 after I noticed that an increasing number of buyers were complaining about tiny imperfections not listed in the auction descriptions. At first I gave the buyers the benefit of the doubt and believed that I must have missed something when examining the pieces. But as the number of complaints increased, I knew something was wrong. When I first began to sell online, I would have one complaint every six weeks, but rapidly the number of complaints had increased to almost one a week.

I happened to see a magazine article about eBay strategies. In this article, the author advised eBay buyers to complain about an item after they'd received it even if the piece was perfect. He further suggested that they threaten negative feedback! The article stated that the seller may offer a discount upon receiving a complaint. It explained that sellers would likely give a partial refund to keep the buyer from returning the item and avoid return shipping costs. I was shocked. This is dishonest and bad for everyone on eBay. It is not fair to the seller, and it is not fair to other bidders who bid on the item.

I went to the local bookstore, flipped through several eBay "how to" books, and found that most of the books gave a similar suggestion. However, most of the other books did not openly recommend such dishonesty. The other books said to look carefully at the piece and see if you can find any flaws not mentioned then complain. The result is still the same for sellers. Many buyers complain about damaged items because they want discounts, not because they are really unhappy with the item. So I started to become more cautious. Before I would offer a reduction in price, I would question the buyer and ask for photographs of the damage. When I did not believe the damage was real or significant, I would tell the buyer just to return the piece for a refund. It has been my experience that over 95 percent of buyers will keep the supposedly damaged item rather than return it for a full refund. I believe this number is so high because there was never anything wrong with the item. If the item is returned, then I can re-list the piece making sure to note any and all damage.

California Scam Artist

We received several high-end cameras from a professional photographer to sell on eBay. The photographer told us he had cleaned and checked out all the equipment prior to bringing it to us, and everything worked fine. So I was suspicious when I received an e-mail from a buyer stating that the camera he had purchased had a minor problem and that it would cost $150 to repair. He stated that I had to pay for this repair or that he would send the camera back. I told him to send it back. He then emailed me and said that he had already taken the camera to be repaired. So I waited until the following morning and called the buyer.

Since he lived in California and there was a three-hour time difference, I decided I may have a better chance at the truth if I caught him early in the morning. When his mother answered the phone and said that he was still asleep, I told her I needed to speak to her son on a very important matter and asked her to please wake him.

A groggy young man answered the phone. I told him who I was and that I was calling about the camera that needed repair. He was apparently a little confused, because he began to talk about a camera that was a different brand than the one I had sold him. I told him that I had sold him the Nikon camera. I found it strange that this young man had purchased two very high-end cameras and both had minor problems.

I asked the young man if he had taken my camera to be repaired. He said that he had, which is why I had to refund him the $150 so he could pay for the repair. I asked him the name of the camera shop. There was a long pause. He asked me why I wanted the name of the camera shop. I told him I was going to contact the camera shop and question the repair person about the camera. He stated that he could not remember the name of the shop. Now, I must admit that I was starting to have a little fun with him because he was obviously not being honest.

"You are telling me that you took a $1000 camera in for repair and you do not know the name of the business?" I asked.

There was another long pause. He said that the camera shop was right down the street from his house, and he just did not remember the name. So then I asked for the address of the camera shop. He did not know the address. I asked for the name of the street. He did not know that either.

"Are you trying to tell me you do not know the name of the street that is down from your house?" I asked.

There was another long pause.

I asked to speak with his mother.

The young man hung up on me instead of putting his mother on the phone. There was never anything wrong with the camera he had purchased from me.

Now intrigued, and with my suspicion confirmed, I decided to do a little detective work. I looked at the buyer's feedback and found that he had purchased a lot of high-end electronics and cameras. I also noticed that he sold a lot of the same high-end electronics and cameras.

Now the puzzle pieces were fitting together. I contacted several of the sellers who had sold to him. Everyone that responded to my emails stated that the buyer had reported a problem with the item, and they had given him some of his money back on the purchase. Some of the sellers gave him as little as $50 and some as much as $250.

I had to give the young man credit for being inventive—he was dishonest, but he was working a very lucrative scam. He would buy high-end electronics and cameras, which have consistent sales prices on eBay. After the purchases, he would complain to the sellers about a nonexistent problem and threaten to return the item and/or give them negative feedback if they did not refund enough to pay for the repairs. He had sought out sellers who dealt in high volume and sold on consignment. Such sellers were less likely to know the product firsthand and more likely to find it easier to refund partial payment than to deal with a return. The young scammer would then resell the item on eBay for approximately the same amount that he had purchased it for and pocket the "repair" money. From the limited data I could collect on him, I estimated that he was turning over two to three items each week. So he was making about $200 to $400 dollars a week for just a few hours of dishonest work.

I reported the problem to eBay, but it is hard for the site to act on this kind of fraud. The evidence I had against the user was circumstantial, and it would be difficult to prove that none of the cameras had had problems. So I decided to take a more direct approach. I called his mother. We had a very long chat about her son's extracurricular activities. She assured me that her son would be making no more eBay purchases. I checked up on that user ID for several weeks, and I found that his mother was as good as her word. There was no more buying or selling by the seventeen-year-old scam artist.

Most of the people you will do business with on eBay will be great people that are honest and easy to work with, but you do need to watch for those few who are not. The site cannot protect you from every dishonest person who frequents it, so you have to protect yourself. We will discuss more on the ethics of buying and selling in chapter nine.

Chapter Six
Reselling Goods for Profit

One of the major benefits that you will gain from using the Flipster System is the ability to generate cash whenever you need it. There are very few jobs or careers that give you the flexibility to increase your earnings or take time off at your own discretion. Daren and I always have plenty of items to list and usually have more items than we have time to get them all listed. If we have an unexpected bill or need some extra cash, we know that we can list extra items to generate the needed cash. Daren refers to it as the legal way to instantly create cash.

Using this system will also give you the freedom to choose how and when you generate your income. If you do not need the extra income or you are leaving for vacation, you can choose to not sell any items. There may be some weeks when you sell only five items and other weeks when you sell fifty items. The choice is yours.

Buying items specifically to resell can be a fun and financially rewarding endeavor. If you decide you want to do this on a full- or part-time basis, you most likely will want to sell your items yourself to eliminate the cost of a trading assistant. However, I do have several part-time dealers for whom I sell. They are able to buy wisely so they can still make a profit even after paying my commission. You may want to consider a trading assistant or drop-off store when you first get started and are building your online reputation. Then you can start selling on your own when you feel you've had enough experience. If you decide to use a trading assistant, be sure you factor in the assistant's commission before you purchase items to resell.

FINDING YOUR PASSION

At this point, I want to sidetrack briefly from the mechanics and focus on the heart or passion of what we do. To resell your own items as your needs change or as you upgrade does not require a love or passion of the business. However, if you decide to buy goods as a moneymaking business, you need to have an interest in, some knowledge of, and a love or passion for what you are selling.

Think about what you are interested in or have knowledge about—everyone has something—and start there. If you love what you are doing, you are more likely to want to invest your time and energy in its pursuit. As you begin to buy and sell a particular type of item that you know or are passionate about (hopefully both), you will gain even more knowledge, and your expertise in your chosen area will grow. Then you can start expanding your buying. You will find that you can have a continuously expanding circle of ever-increasing knowledge and informed buying. Recall the woman who started purchasing designer jeans for resale and wound up branching out.

Let me share another example of how a passion can turn into a profitable hobby. Let's say a person is a collector of Lionel trains. He enjoys the trains, and as a collector, he is very knowledgeable on the subject of Lionel trains. He starts using the Flipster System by selling the part of his collection that he no longer wants. Then he starts to purchase Lionel trains and accessories specifically for resale. As he buys and resells Lionel trains, he comes in contact with other types of model or toy trains. He begins to make small purchases of Marx, Tyco, and Marklin trains. His knowledgebase begins to grow, and he feels more comfortable buying. He now can tell the difference between a high-quality train and a low-quality train without looking at the maker's name. This knowledgebase continues to grow as he comes in contact with other model toys. Soon he is buying and selling model trains, cars, and other items. His knowledgebase can continue to grow as far as he wants to pursue it. He can learn about all types of toys or decide to expand into other areas.

Most people have more than one area of interest or knowledge, so you can see how this ever-increasing circle could grow rapidly in only a few months. If you put yourself out in the world as a seeker of information and knowledge, you will find it. You should begin buying items that you know, but do not limit yourself to just those areas. Be open to new interests and areas of knowledge. I have found through the years that my interests and focus have changed as I've been exposed to new types of items that are excellent prospects for resale.

The great thing about this business is that one person can never know everything about everything. There is a never-ending array of items that are as diverse as humanity itself, and the more you know about them, the better your ability to purchase wisely. Also the more you expose yourself to other areas, the more likely you are to increase your passion or find new passions. Some people have jobs that pay a great deal of money, and other people have jobs that they enjoy or that fulfill them. Ideally with the Flipster System, you can make a great deal of money at a job that you find both fulfilling and enjoyable.

What not to do: When Bad Things Happen to Stupid People

An older woman came into our drop-off store with three large boxes full of jewelry. She stated that she had purchased this jewelry on eBay and had tried to sell it at the local flea market over the last few months but had had little success and could not understand why. She wanted me to try to sell it on eBay so she could recoup some of her money.

It is very hard to buy something on eBay and resell it on eBay to make a profit. Occasionally you will find a person who lists something so badly or incorrectly that you are able to get a good deal. Sometimes you are also able to find huge lots then break them up into smaller auctions. This woman stated that the jewelry was all high-quality gold, diamonds, and gemstones. When I opened up the first box, I immediately knew that this woman had no idea what she had purchased. She obviously knew nothing about fine jewelry.

All the jewelry was cheap, dollar-store jewelry made overseas in China and Hong Kong. None of the jewelry was real gold. None of the jewelry had real diamonds or gemstones. The jewelry was so bad and so cheap I did not need to look at the pieces with a jeweler's loop to know they were garbage. You could see with a naked eye that the quality was poor; the settings were base metal with gold-toned plating and the stones looked like they came from a gumball machine, not a jewelry store. I knew I was going to have to be the bearer of very bad news.

I tried to show the woman that the stones were plastic and the metal was not gold but merely gold-toned. She would not believe me. She stated that she had purchased this all from a very nice person on eBay, and he had guaranteed everything was genuine gemstones, diamonds, and gold. She insisted that everything was real. I told her that I was sorry but that I could not help her and she should go back to this person on eBay and try to get her money back. I asked her about the eBay seller and how much money she had paid to him. The woman told me that she had been buying from this seller for over three months, but had not purchased anything in the last two months since she could not sell what she had. She said the seller was based in Hong Kong and that she had paid him over $5,000.

I told her she had been deceived and she should contact eBay right away, because the jewelry she had was worth almost nothing. She was furious with me and thought I was somehow trying to defraud her even though I refused to take any of her jewelry. Two days later, she came back to my store stating that she had contacted eBay, but it was too late because the seller was no longer a registered eBay user. No doubt due to fraud, eBay had removed the seller. Since the dishonest seller lived overseas, if the woman were to go to court and win a judgment against him, she would be very unlikely to collect.

Mistakes to Avoid

The woman in the story above made three common mistakes that first-time sellers can easily avoid:

- Don't purchase items you know nothing about. This woman obviously had never seen a high-quality piece of jewelry in her life, and she had no knowledge or experience in the jewelry industry.

- Don't invest a lot of money in an untested market. The woman in our story invested too much-money, I might add, that she could not afford to lose. She was on a fixed income, and her husband was only working part time. If she had wanted to try to buy on eBay to resell at the flea market, she should have purchased $100 worth of goods. She would have learned the same lesson, but instead of losing $5000 dollars, she would have only been out $100. I cannot emphasize enough the importance of starting out small and refraining from making any large investments without testing the market first.

- Know the markets. Don't make purchases on a higher market to resell at a lower market. Most items sold at flea markets receive less money than items sold on eBay. So she was selling down and not up. Our section on sourcing will help you to find great places to buy and sell your merchandise. Everyone will make purchasing mistakes from time to time, but you must limit your risk, especially when you are a beginner and learning about the products and markets.

STARTUP CAPITAL NOT NEEDED

Another great thing about reselling online is that very little startup capital is needed. This is a great side business for young mothers, retirees, part-timers, and hobbyists. The prudent way to start a reselling business is to start reselling for yourself and then expand into selling for others.

As with any new venture, we suggest that you start slow and be frugal. If you have a good computer and a digital camera, there is no need to buy better ones right away. Use the equipment you have until you start making a profit; then reinvest in your business.

If and when the time comes that you want to open up a drop-off store, be sure you have enough capital saved to last you several months, because your business will not take off right away. There is no need to rent a huge space or a fancy location. Also, do not buy new, expensive office equipment. New businesses have a high failure rate, because the owners overextend themselves. They take out business loans for unnecessary and extravagant items. Many sign contracts with franchise companies and must pay franchise fees and adhere to costly rules of the franchise.

I know there are drop-off store franchises all over the country ready to make you part of their companies, but that may not be the best avenue for success. There are a few profitable drop-off franchises, but there are many that are making money solely off selling franchises and not by selling on eBay. The drop-off store model is not one of high profit, and with the extra fees involved with a franchise, I find it hard to believe many new franchise owners will make it past their first year. It is almost impossible to have a profitable business selling for others unless you sell for yourself too. At the time of printing, we have seen six drop-off franchise stores close in the Raleigh, North Carolina, area since we started our business just four years ago.

STARTING OUT FRUGALLY

When we began to resell items for other people, we operated out of our home. Soon we had saved up $5,000, and we decided to open up a drop-off location. We could have easily gone to our bank and received a loan to purchase new furniture, office equipment, shelving, and lobby room furniture, but of course we did not. We wanted our new offices to look nice so customers would feel comfortable using our services, but we did not want to go into debt setting up the office. We moved my home office furniture into my new office space and moved our home computer to the office. We found a company that was going out of business and purchased their lobby furniture for a fraction of the retail cost. I remember the owner said that he had paid a great deal of money for the furniture. I am sure that is true. It was very nice, and since he was in business less than a year, it looked brand new. I also remember that the owner told me he was going out of business because of too much overhead. I have no doubt that is true too. You can have a great business and generate tons of cash, but if the cash is leaving the business as fast as it is coming in the door, you will not be in business for long.

We also needed sturdy shelving to hold all the goods waiting to be sold. So we went to a place that sells secondhand office equipment and supplies. We purchased just enough shelving to get us started. We did not need to fill the entire back room with shelving since we had a very small customer base. We knew that eventually we would come across more shelving that was even less expensive from a distressed seller. We shopped around for the best deals on boxes and packing material. We also negotiated with the top three shipping companies to get a deal on our shipping costs.

As we became known in the community, and news of our service spread, we began to get more and more customers. We needed another computer, and we purchased one that was less than a year old from another company that was closing its doors. We added paintings and prints to our lobby as we were able to purchase them for a few dollars at yard sales. Basically, as we grew, we added the things we needed to facilitate or to spur growth. We never went into debt and never paid retail for anything in our offices. I want to add here that our offices never looked like a thrift store but more like a high-end lawyer's office. We furnished the office with current goods on the market mixed with some antiques since we specialize in selling antiques. Our offices looked better than the offices of many who had paid thousands for similarly-sized work places.

After we'd had our drop-off store for about a year and a half, we decided we had accomplished what we'd wanted to do. We had wanted to get our name out into the community and establish ourselves as a reliable eBay reseller. We'd wanted to expand our customer base so that we would always have as much business as we wanted.

Daren and I talked about either growing the business more or taking it down to a smaller size and back to a home-based business. We had several serious offers to franchise eBizAuctions and several offers of financial backing to help us expand. I wanted to spend more time with our daughter and more time doing all the other things I loved to do. So we decided to take the business back into our home. Our home at the time was over thirty minutes away from our customer base, and it was not set up for a large home-based business. So we found a centrally located house that was perfect for a home-based business with an office up front and a large garage for storage.

Our move out of the office and into this new home turned out great. We purchased a much larger home in a better location and reinvested in our major asset instead of paying rent on a retail space. We now have less overhead and more space, and we are investing in our property asset. Since over 95 percent of my customers come from referral or repeat customers, I have maintained the same customer levels, but I have scaled down the amount of merchandise that I will take. Since I work out of my home, I have no commuting expenses or all the other expenses that add up when you are working away from home. I am able to set my own work schedule so I am home when our daughter arrives from school, and I have much more free time to do the things I love while earning a nice income.

Chapter Seven
How and What to Buy

In the previous chapter we spoke about selling the items you have in your closets and attics in order to get started or to recoup some of your investments and purchase new assets. Some of you may be happy stopping at this point, because you have unloaded your unwanted assets and made some money to put toward new purchases. That is great, and you will find that the next time you feel the need to upgrade your electronics, sports equipment, or any assets, you will again return to the Flipster System in order to make the most of your purchases.

There will be many of you who have found the Flipster System to be an eye-opening experience and are eager to try your hand at buying for the sole purpose of reselling. Keep in mind that using the Flipster System to buy and resell can be a part-time or full-time adventure. When we started out twenty years ago, both Daren and I had full time corporate jobs and only did our "flipping" as the opportunity presented itself.

The next step to becoming a reseller is to decide what you want to start selling. Again, I want to state that you should always start with what you know and grow from that point. When you decide to sell, be sure to research your market. And no matter what you decide to sell, you will need to find places to buy and sell your items.

We have discussed selling online at length, but that is not *always* the best or only place to sell items. We discuss and reference eBay a great deal in this book, because it is a good place to sell your goods, but, more importantly, it is an *easy* place to sell. Sites like eBay give the average person access to millions of shoppers every day, which is crucial to a reseller. Although the online marketplace is a great place to sell goods, we sell many items through local auction houses. It is your job as a reseller to find the best markets to not only buy but to sell your goods. Chapter eleven is dedicated to providing a plethora of sourcing options, but you will need to investigate each option in your local area to know where you can obtain the highest profit margin.

For example, when we purchase an estate or storage unit full of goods, we go through each box and divide up the goods according to where and when we will resell them.

We also divide the junk items into a donation pile and a pile that will go to the dump. Do not waste your time on items that should be taken to the local dump.

Some of the good items we put aside for eBay and others we pack up to send to a local auction house. There are several competitive auction houses in our area. We are frequent customers, and we have learned which specialized buyers attend which auctions. There is one auction house near our home that has several silver dealers competing with each other on the high-end silver, especially southern sterling and coin silver. That type of silver sells better at this particular auction house than it does on eBay. So when I have this type of silver, I resell it at that auction house.

However, that same auction house does not sell antique furniture well at all. On occasion we have been able to buy a piece of furniture at this auction house and drive it across town and sell it at another auction house, which has many furniture dealers as regular customers. We've been able to make a nice profit after paying the auctioneer's commission! Being able to make a profit in a situation like that depends on years of experience and knowledge of your local market. I would not attempt a flip like this until you have had a great deal of experience buying and reselling in your local market.

We also have a storage shelf that holds all the left over things that are not "good" enough for eBay or auctions, but are still items of value. We hold these items until we have enough for a huge yard sale, which we usually do only twice a year so as not to drive the neighbors crazy. We always make at least a thousand dollars at each sale.

As to divvying up items according to *when* you should sell them, remember that, when possible, you want to buy during the off-season and sell during the in-season. We once purchased the inventory of a sporting goods store that was going out of business. We sold the swimsuits right away since it was summertime, but we stored the skiing equipment for several months until the beginning of ski season.

EDUCATING YOURSELF

We have talked about finding your niche or your passion and beginning your selling experiences within those boundaries, but to increase your potential to find goods, you need to broaden your knowledge. As you go forth looking for goods to resell, the wider your area of knowledge, the more you will find to sell. That is why you want to continue to educate yourself in as many areas as you can. I have always said that we are "jacks of all trades and masters of none;" that is the kind of knowledge we need to succeed in what we do.

Imagine two rivers: one is very wide and shallow, and one is very narrow and deep. In this type of business, you need to be the river that is wide and shallow. *You want to know a little bit about as many areas as possible, but you do not have to have in-depth knowledge in a lot of areas.* You need to be able to spot quality and the names or makers that sell well while in the field; then you can research the rest once you get home. Naturally, you are going to have more depth of knowledge in some areas or specialize in your passion areas, but you should force yourself to branch out to other areas. It is great to have depth of knowledge, but that is a different specialty than what you need to be a Flipster.

In the first appendix, you will find a list of common name brands, makers, and hallmarks sorted by category. In each category, we will sort these names by good, better, and best for resale. This will be an invaluable tool as you begin to search for items for resale. It should be your first but not your only guide to how much you should pay for an item or if you should purchase it at all. There are literally hundreds of thousands of manufacturers of goods, and we could not possibly list them all, so we have also included at the top of each category brief tips for purchasing items in that list. However, there are some general guidelines that are applicable to anything you purchase.

CONDITION, CONDITION, CONDITION

You may have heard the real estate joke that states that the three most important aspects when selling a house are location, location, location. A similar thing can be said about reselling assets: the three most important aspects are condition, condition, condition. The overall condition of an item will play a huge role in how much value a buyer will place on it.

The condition of an item is relative to each item. A small chip on a rare porcelain vase that is one hundred years old may affect the value a little, but a small chip on an average china plate made ten years ago makes that piece almost worthless. An antique item is expected to have some wear, and normal wear usually does not take away from its value. But there is a difference between wear and damage. Wear is what happens to an old piece while it is being used, such as a worn spine and corners on an old book. Damage would be tears in the pages or writing on the cover. The general rule is to stay away from damaged goods unless the item is rare and the damage is minor.

If you are selling modern-day items such as clothing, electronics, or sports equipment, even minor wear can greatly affect the value. If people are going to buy a used item that is still available in the retail stores, they want an item that is in excellent or new condition. There are people who search eBay for used items to use as repair parts, but do not expect to get good prices for those types of items.

QUALITY SELLS

In good times and even in hard times, quality will always sell. If you are going to have any hope for success in this business, you must teach yourself to spot a quality piece. The best way to spot a quality piece is to look at the details. It does not matter if you are looking at clothing, porcelain, or glass, the quality or lack thereof will show if you look for details.

When looking at clothing, you want to look at the stitching and the material. On quality items the stitching should be close together and straight. The material should be fine weave and made of natural fibers such as silk or cotton. The exception would be the new athletic clothing made from high tech fabrics which are synthetic but expensive.

On porcelain items, you should look for delicate details. If the piece is of a human form, look at the face and hands to see how they are sculpted or painted. Look to see if attention was given to every aspect of the piece, even the background.

On glass items, you can use your hands to feel if the glass is cut or pressed. Cut glass, which usually indicates that the piece is of higher quality, will feel sharp to the touch, and pressed glass will not. Also, on glass you can look to see if there is a pontil (the round indention or mark that a glass blower's rod leaves on the bottom of an item), which would indicate that the piece is blown by hand—a sign of quality. A pontil can be rough or it can be polished smooth by grinding. A polished pontil is usually more desirable.

The examples above are simply intended to give you a few ideas of what you should be looking at in your purchases. There will be many details to consider. Many of the items you will encounter will have the manufacturer's name listed on them somewhere, and knowing manufacturers will be a great help to determine the value of an item. However, you will come across items with unfamiliar names or no name at all. If you do not know how to spot quality, then you will either miss out on a great buy or purchase an inferior item for too much money

The Amish Quilt

I was selling some items for a very nice couple who were downsizing. The woman unpacked a quilt and told me that she had purchased it at an antique store while she was on vacation a few years ago. She also told me that it was sold to her as an antique and had been made by the Amish. I could tell from across the room that the quilt was not antique since it did not have any age to it at all. I took a closer look at the quilt and also discovered that it was machine sewn. I hated to break the bad news to the woman, but I had no choice. I asked her how much she'd paid for the quilt and she stated she'd paid $800. I showed her the stitching on the quilt, which was all perfectly uniform and clearly made by a machine. I pointed out that many of the fabric squares were a poly-cotton blend and the batting in the middle was hard and scratchy like a poor synthetic blend. I then gave her the bad news, but I could tell by the look in her eyes that she realized her mistake.

The antique dealer was either uninformed or dishonest, but if the woman had looked at the details, she would not have been taken advantage of by the dealer's lack of knowledge or integrity. The Amish do not sew their quilts by machines, and a quilt that is one hundred years old would have some kind of wear and age showing no matter how well it had been cared for over the years.

The moral of this story is that you should think, look, and feel for yourself and never let your emotions or a sleek salesperson make a purchasing decision for you.

TOOLS OF THE TRADE

There are several important tools of the trade that you'll need to take with you on your searches for treasures. The first and most important is cash. Cash is king when it comes to purchasing, especially in negotiation situations. (Read more about negotiations in chapter eight.) There are many times when the only form of payment the owner will accept is cold, hard cash. Yard sales, flea markets, police auctions, and storage unit auctions almost exclusively deal in cash-only sales.

Some other great items to have are a tape measure, a flash light, a black light, and a Swiss army knife. You never know when you will want to measure an item or be in a place where the lighting is not sufficient. A flash light is also good for looking down into a pot or piece of pottery. Shining a strong light down into a piece can reveal cracks and other damage that can affect the item's value. While a black light is not convenient for taking on some purchasing trips, it can reveal cracks and sometimes repairs. The Swiss army knife has all those great little tools that can come in handy in countless situations.

A jeweler's loop (a small magnifying glass used by jewelers) or a magnifying glass is great thing to have while on your search. A jeweler's loop is invaluable when purchasing jewelry, but it also comes in handy for reading small hallmarks on items like sterling silver. If you intend to purchase jewelry, then you may also want to invest in a gram scale and a diamond tester. These are not expensive items, and both can be purchased on eBay. A very good gram scale should cost less than $50, and a diamond tester can be found for approximately $100. Most diamond testers will not test for Moissanite, lab-created diamonds. In order to test for Moissanite, you must have a special Moissanite tester. A Moissanite stone will have a delicate, very-hard-to-see greenish tint to the stone, which can only be seen with the loop and is usually only detected by professional jewelers.

A good pair of shoes will serve you well when you are walking the seemingly endless miles of the flea market or when you are jumping in and out of the car while yard-sale shopping.

Since we are on the subject of clothing, be sure to dress appropriately when you're out bargain hunting. You want use basic psychology to your benefit when on buying trips. People feel more comfortable around people like themselves and are more willing to sell their goods at bargain prices to people who make them feel comfortable. So do not dress like you are a millionaire, fresh off the yacht and dripping in diamonds and gold. It will be hard to bargain down a price if you look as though you have a lot of extra cash to spend. However, you do not want to look like you have no money. The seller may feel uncomfortable or may feel they are wasting their time dealing with someone who cannot afford to purchase any of their items.

SMART RISK, DUMB RISK

There will come a time when you will see an opportunity you believe to be a real moneymaker, but you will not be sure if you're instinct is right. As I have said many times before, no one person can know everything about everything in this business, and sometimes you just have to take a risk. But you do not have to take dumb risks. The trick is to know the difference between the two.

As a beginner I would advise not risking any more than you are prepared to lose, because you will make bad investments, and that is part of the learning process. As you delve further into this line of work, bigger and better opportunities will come your way, and you must gauge how much you are prepared to risk in order to achieve real gains.

Buying known items at a price you know will generate profit is no risk at all and therefore the easiest and best type of purchase to make. Buying an item that is unknown to you but has quality and is in excellent condition at a reasonable price is a smart risk. Buying an item sight unseen, at a high price, or based upon what some unknown person is telling you is a dumb risk.

Eastlake Plant Stand

One night Daren and I were sitting at an auction when an Eastlake plant stand with a marble top came up for auction. I had given it a cursory look while examining other items but had not really considered buying it. It was a quality piece with lovely architectural design elements, which I was sure would make it a sought-after item in the auction. I just assumed the piece would go at too high a price for me to consider buying it. When the item went up for auction, I was surprised to see it about to sell for only $50, so I jumped into the bidding at the very last moment and was able to buy the piece for only $60. We do not deal in a lot of furniture, mainly because it is heavy to haul around, so I am not as familiar or comfortable buying furniture as I am buying other types of goods. However, this piece was small and of good quality, so I decided to take the risk. When I returned home, I searched for similar items on eBay and found that this type of plant stand sells for between $300 and $450. I have so far chosen not to profit from my risk-taking auction purchase, because the plant stand looks very nice in my office. However, if I choose to sell it, I am confident I will receive a nice return on my investment.

This is an example of Eastlake furniture popular during the Victorian period. The Eastlake style is named after Charles Eastlake, designer.

Because I recognized the Eastlake style and the quality of the piece, I realized that a great deal had presented itself when the stand was about to sell so low. The ability to recognize names of international and national brands is important, but name recognition of local products is equally important. *Learn about famous artists who reside in your area or things that are popular locally. These will be the items you come across most often.*

A Gnome by Any Other Name

My purchase of two Tom Clark gnomes at a tag sale is not only a great example of smart risk taking, but it shows how you can apply a wide but shallow knowledge. I had become familiar with Tom Clark gnomes, because I had seen them several times at estate sales and auction houses, and I had also sold the gnomes several times for customers here in Raleigh, North Carolina. The sculptor, Tom Clark resides near Raleigh in Elizabeth Town, so naturally there are many collectors in North Carolina and many examples of his work locally. Tom Clark may be a local artist but his fans can be found as far away as England and Japan.

My past experience had taught me that some of these gnomes can bring several hundred dollars, but others will sell for as little as $5. Since my knowledge was shallow, I did not know if these two gnomes were the $5- or the hundreds of dollars-variety.

This is where calculated risk became a factor. There are literally hundreds of versions of these gnomes, and only a collector or an expert would be able to know the value of any one gnome without doing a little research. But in the middle of a tag sale, you do not have the time to stop to research an item. You have to make a quick, onsite decision whether the risk is acceptable or not. Each gnome was $15, so to me it was an easy decision; even if the gnomes were worthless, I would only be out $30, and the potential to make money was great.

I took the gnomes home with me and found that I had been quite lucky. I sold both of the gnomes the next week on eBay for a combined total of $351.

About two months later, I found three more Tom Clark gnomes at another tag sale. Again, the gnomes were from the early 1980s and in perfect condition, so I grabbed them up and happily paid $40 for the lot. Imagine my disappointment when none of the three gnomes were worth very much at all. I sold all three in one eBay auction for $30. Although I lost money on the deal, I still think it was an appropriate risk to take. You can't win on every deal, and when I combine the totals from all five gnomes, I am still way ahead.

Tom Clark sculptures prices vary from ten dollars to several thousand dollars on eBay.

This next example demonstrates how listening to your instincts can help you avoid dumb risks. A storage unit auction occurs when the renter of the unit does not pay the rent on the unit and the owner of the storage facility sells off the contents of the unit in order to pay for past due rent. What the owner of the facility is really looking to do is clean out the unit so he can rent it to a paying customer. Normally what happens in this situation is that the lock to the unit is cut and potential buyers have a short period of time to look over the contents of the unit before the bidding begins. I attended a storage unit auction that was run by an auctioneer whom I'd had no prior experience with, and this gentleman ran his auction quite differently.

Avoid Behind-the-Curtain Deals

About two years ago, I was at a storage unit auction where the contents of the unit were sold sight unseen. The locks on the doors were not cut until after the bidding was over! I have been to enough of these auctions to know that the contents of a storage unit can vary greatly—from hundreds of boxes filled with china and collectibles to nothing but a couple of boxes of personal papers worth nothing. Also, I got the feeling that something was not right about this auction and this situation. Sometimes it is best to listen to your gut feeling, especially if it is telling you something is wrong. If your instincts are screaming at you to beware, then it is better to be safe than sorry later. Needless to say, I was not willing to risk any of my money without at least a little peek into the unit. I felt like I was on the old game show, "Let's Make a Deal," and I was being asked to choose a prize that was hidden behind a curtain. But I got the distinct impression that the only person who would be walking away a winner was the auctioneer.

I stuck around long enough to see that there was very little in any of the units, and it is my guess that the auctioneer and storage unit owner must have known that in advance or they would not have had such an unorthodox auction.

It is human nature to want to walk away with a purchase after you have invested your time in an auction, but do not let your emotions get you into a bad situation. Keep in mind one of the key Flipster philosophies: there is always more. There is always another auction or another yard sale. Sometimes it is best to walk away.

BANK ROLLING: FINANCING YOUR PURCHASES

The great thing about this system is you do not have to have a lot of startup cash. You can start small and build your capital through the resale of your inventory. You do not need a retail store, expensive equipment, or supplies. This whole process can and should be done out of your own home with very little upfront money. If your finances are really tight, you can start out by selling your own unwanted items to make some starting capital. Or you could start with ten or twenty dollars and shop at some local yard sales. Resell those items and reinvest your profits into more items. It would be a good idea to continue to reinvest your profits back into your purchases until you have a nice bank roll so you can afford to pay for nice, high-quality items when the opportunity presents itself. Below is an example of how the reinvesting of your profits could create your bank roll for the business.

Let us say you have made all the upfront preparations to sell online such as getting an ID and setting up a seller's account with eBay, and you are now prepared to start selling merchandise online. You look around your house and find you have a couple of McCoy vases and an old Sony stereo you do not use. You list those on eBay, and combined, the auctions total $75. Remember you have to pay eBay and PayPal fees of an estimated $8, which leaves you with a net total of $67.

The next weekend you take your $67 dollars and shop at the local yard sales. Take $10 off for gas to drive around. When you first start out, be sure to make small, conservative purchases so you do not waste your start up money. The time to take risks will come later. (To make this example as realistic as possible, I am going to use actual examples of things Daren and I have purchased at yard sales during one average weekend and what we actually sold them for on eBay a few weeks later.)

Your purchases for the weekend include a lot of vintage Hot Wheels cars in very used condition, two Royal Doulton plates, two O'Neil wetsuits, a vintage McCoy cookie jar, and a Spyder paintball gun. On these purchases, you spend a total of $33. You sell the lot of Hot Wheel cars for $21.50, the Royal Doulton plates for $30.05, the O'Neil wetsuits for $20.50 and $14.99, the McCoy Circus Horse Cookie Jar for $76.99, and the Spyder paintball gun for $32.51.

Your gross sales total ($196.54) less your original investment ($33) and your eBay expenses ($18) leaves you with a net sales total of $145.54. You still have $34 dollars left over from your original $67, so that brings your earnings to $179.54. You take out another $20 for packing material. (Some very frugal people are able to go to stores and other places to get free boxes and packing material, but I just do not have the time. However, if you are only shipping a few items a week, it may be worth your time.)

You have gone from having zero investment money to $159.54 in just two weeks. Please keep in mind I used real examples—those were the actual prices we paid for the items and the actual amounts we resold them for, so anyone can do this.

You want to continue to multiply your cash until you get to a point where you have enough bank roll money, and then you can start to pay yourself. So to continue with this example, let's say you reinvest your $159.54 in more items, and eventually you have a bank roll of $450. It is good to have at least $300 to $500 in cash with you when you are going to flea markets or yard sales. If you are attending storage facility auctions or police auction, keep in mind that many of them require cash only, so you may want to have a little more on hand if possible. Local or estate auctions usually take checks and credit cards, but I always like to pay in cash. You do not want to be putting your purchases on your credit card unless you know you can pay the balance off right away without any interest payments. Paying interest on a credit card would negate any profits you make.

So let's say you are satisfied with a bank roll of $300. Keep the $300 aside, and pay yourself the extra $150 you have earned. Now you are buying with "free money." I use the term free money to describe the money you have earned through smart buying and reselling. After you become comfortable with purchasing small, inexpensive items to resell, start to expand what you are willing to purchase and look for high-end luxury goods. You do have to spend money to make money in this business. Be sure to learn about as many items as you can so you can widen your area of knowledge. If you started with yard-sale and flea-market purchases, expand your buying to all the different kinds of auctions available in your area. Start to take smart, calculated risks when buying. Do not forget to explore other sales channels for your items too. It is important to purchase wisely, but it is equally important to sell at the best place possible.

YOUR BANK ROLL AND SEASONAL ITEMS

I usually try to move my purchases as soon as possible. It makes sense to turn your money over as fast as you can, especially if you are dealing with technological items. Technology changes so rapidly that a product that is only six months old can be out of date. Always try to move your electronics and technology-based items as quickly as possible.

I have mentioned before that you should try to buy in the off-season and sell in the in-season. But doing this could affect your bank roll. If you come across a store closing or another great opportunity to purchase seasonal items, you may have to hold these items for a short or long period of time before you can sell them for maximum profit. You will have to weigh maximizing your profit against keeping your cash tied up in assets you cannot sell right away. It may not be in your best interest to hold assets for a long period of time if the gain would not outweigh the loss of the use of the capital that is tied up in the assets.

For instance, let's say that I purchased three hundred Hallmark Christmas ornaments in February for a fantastic deal. Of course the best time to resell those ornaments would be in the months and weeks before next Christmas, but that would mean that my money would be tied up for ten months. I would also have to store those items somewhere for ten months, and I have a limited storage space. I would never consider paying for storage. All my profit would be eaten up in storage fees. So is it a good idea to keep these ornaments around for ten months? Everyone's situation is different, but I would be inclined to sell them right away. However, if I had purchased the ornaments in September, I would be more willing to wait just a few months for the potentially higher profit.

Chapter Eight
The Power of Negotiation

NEGOTIATE EVERY DAY

Negotiation is a skill that must be practiced to be perfected. Many people are intimidated or afraid to negotiate even the simplest of deals. Keep in mind that the definition of negotiation is *a discussion intended to produce an agreement.* Everyone has hundreds of discussions every day. Whether you realize it or not, you negotiate with your family, friends, and coworkers on just about every topic imaginable: what movie to see; how late your teenager can stay out at night; what restaurant you will dine at.

Each of us will instinctively negotiate day-to-day decisions with those closest to us. It is an automatic and unconscious activity. What we want to teach you is to bring out this ability, sharpen this skill, and broaden the situations where you can use this talent.

FEAR OF REJECTION

One of the biggest road blocks people have in starting a negotiation is the fear of rejection. Most people especially have the fear of the big NO. There is no doubt you will hear this answer, but in this chapter we have included our tips and techniques that will give you the power to avoid the no and get the best price you can for your purchase. Actually, if you do not get told no on occasion, you are most likely not bargaining hard enough. Getting a no response is not the worst thing that can happen during a transaction. The seller walking away from the negotiation is the worst thing that can happen. What we will do in this chapter is teach you how to negotiate a great deal without offending the seller—one where everyone walks away from the table feeling like a winner.

He Who Names a Price First, Loses

To get the upper hand, a good negotiator should try to get the other person to name a price first. Be sure to access the situation, be subtle in your approach and never insult the seller. Below are some phrases you can use to opening the dialogue with a potential seller.

- What is your best price on this item?
- Can you do any better on the price?
- If I buy more than one item, will you lower the price?
- I usually pay a lot less for this item, are you willing to negotiate the price?
- What are you looking to get for this item?

There will come a time when you are trying to start a negotiation and the seller throws the ball back in your court by telling you to make an offer. You do not want the negotiation to get competitive, hostile, or tense. So when someone tells you to make an offer, use a trick that a friend of mine who is a pawnbroker taught me: give the seller an incredibly lowball price. One of two things will happen; the seller will be shocked and say that the item is worth at least "X" amount of dollars, or he or she will take the offer.

If the former happens, you have a place to start your negotiations. Your reply should be surprise—you had no idea that the item was worth so much. Then begin to negotiate a better price than what the seller stated the item was worth. Keep in mind that you do not want to offend the seller, so never make snide or rude remarks. If the seller's idea of value is completely off the reality charts, you may be better off searching elsewhere for deals and not wasting your time on this seller.

On the other hand, sometimes the seller will take the lowball offer. There have been many times that I have offered a dollar or two for an item worth a great deal more, and the owner has taken the offer. Sometimes sellers are only interested in ridding themselves of the item. They may not need the money or care about receiving a fair compensation.

I should note at this point that there are circumstances where ethics play a role in what we do. We will discuss the ethics of buying for resale in chapter nine. However, it's important to mention that when Daren or I are acting as a professional appraiser or a professional dealer, we have a much higher standard than when we are out searching for bargains at a yard sale or flea market. You never want to take advantage of someone who is in a vulnerable position, but you should not feel obligated to tell fully functional adults that they are selling their goods way below market value.

PRACTICE, PRACTICE, PRACTICE

There are some daily activities such as driving your car or brushing your teeth that you have done so often you perform the function automatically and without thinking. At some point you had to learn to perform these functions and practice to refine these skills.

Think back to when you were in driver's education class and how awkward and uncomfortable you felt behind the wheel of the car. When you were first learning, driving took concentration and mental effort, but now you can hop in your car and drive to the local grocery without a thought.

Those of you who have never been actively involved in negotiations may at first flounder and feel inept, but you must persevere. After practicing and becoming successful in a few bargaining situations, you will see how easy it is. Hopefully, you will get to a point where discussing the price of things will become automatic and second nature. There are certain goods and services that can never be negotiated such as your electric bill and most retail store items (there are exceptions there too), but we have found that you can potentially bargain about just about everything else.

ASSESS THE SITUATION

The difference between a good negotiator and a great negotiator is that the great ones assess the situation before they begin their negotiations. You want to look for clues that will tip you off as to when, where, and with whom you should negotiate. You do not have to be a detective or even an intuitive person to see the clues in front of you. You do need to be observant and practiced at this skill so that it becomes automatic and second nature to you.

Clues Amid the Ferns

Daren and I needed to buy some ferns to put in our house for a photo shoot. We were having a picture taken at our home for an *Entrepreneur Magazine* story. We stopped at a roadside stand that was selling fruit and plants. The two attendants were casually relaxing in the fruit stand area, and neither made any effort to wait on us while we were examining the plants. Most of the plants appeared to be healthy, but some were in need of water. There was a handwritten sign near the ferns that stated the price as $10 each or $29 dollars for three.

While I picked out the best two ferns, I asked Daren to go make a deal on the two, because I did not need three, and I was certainly going to ask for more than a dollar off the single-purchase price. Daren went to the clerk and said that we only wanted two ferns. He then asked the clerk what the best deal he could offer for just the two plants. The clerk said that he did not want to pack up the plants later so he would sell them both for $10.

The original price, $10 for each fern was a fair price, but $5 each (50 percent off the asking price) was a great price. Daren paid the man, and we took our ferns without trying to force the issue or beat the price down even lower. We got a great deal, and the clerk was happy to have sold the plants, leaving both buyer and seller with a good feeling.

Before we leave this example, I want to draw your attention to the question Daren asked the clerk. He asked the clerk what was the best deal he could offer. That question put the setting of the price with the clerk. To be honest, I would have paid the $20 for the two ferns, and I would have asked the clerk to sell me both of them for $15 (and happily paid it), never suspecting that he would offer to sell both ferns for the price of one. So by not setting the price myself, I saved $10. If Daren had asked the clerk if he would take $15 for the ferns, it is unlikely that the clerk would have rejected the offer and counter-offered to sell us the pair for just $10.

Just as a good detective picks up on clues to solve a crime, you can pick up on the subtle hints that will identify negotiation opportunities. Listed below are the signs that alerted us to the fact that this may be an opportunity for negotiation.

1.　The two sales clerks did not approach us, which threw up a flag that this was a pretty casual operation without hard core salespeople.

2.　Although the plants were in good shape, the lack of watering indicated there was not a great emphasis placed on caring for the merchandise. If the owners continued to neglect the plants, they would have to trash what they didn't sell, so we figured they might be willing to take whatever they could get for their items.

3.　Because the sellers offered three plants for a lower price than one, we knew they would be agreeable to negotiation.

4.   Also, knowing the seasonal market of plants, we knew that by midsummer in the south, people are not as eager to buy plants. In fact, we would not have been shopping for plants if it had not been for the photo opportunity.

CHOOSE THE RIGHT PERSON

Sometimes there is only one person holding the yard sale or attending the booth at a flea market, so you will have no choice as to who to deal with, but in many situations there is more than one person. How do you know who is the best person to approach to get the best price? The answer is simple—whoever is *not* the owner of the goods. The owner of the goods is always going to think the goods are worth more than anyone else. He or she knows what the item cost new and may have a sentimental attachment to the item.

For example, if a husband and wife are running a yard sale, and I want to buy some tools that are displayed, I would go to the wife, because most likely the tools belong to the husband. She sees them as junk they have had around the house for years, and she has never seen her husband use them, so he must not need them. To her, they are some old tools that are taking up space in the garage, and she wants to get rid of them quickly. But to her husband, they are useful and expensive tools, which are in like-new condition, because he has rarely used them. Perspective plays a key role in determining price. Sometimes the wife will shout over to the husband and ask him for a price. If that happens, just grimace a little and then offer her a quarter to a half off the stated price. Most of the time, the spouse you are dealing with will take the offer before his or her mate has a chance to come over and refuse.

Conversely, if I have my eye on a set of china, I would try to go to the husband, because most likely he has little to do with selecting the china. He sees the china as some old dishes that have been packed away and unused for years. However, the wife remembers the china from Thanksgiving dinners at her grandmother's, so her sentiment toward the dishes will affect her asking price.

Other times you will have a situation where there is one person at the sale or booth who is keen to move the merchandise and another who is more interested in getting top dollar for the goods. The best way to determine who is ready to deal and who is not is to listen to the conversations each salesperson has while you are browsing the items. Listen to both sellers as they deal with other buyers at the sale. It will become obvious within just a few minutes which seller is willing to cut prices in order to move the merchandise.

BUY IN BULK

If you go to a great yard sale, flea market, or antique store where there are multiple items you want to purchase, be sure to ask for and expect a bulk discount. Do not buy things you do not want just to get a bulk discount, but if there are several good items, be sure to let the seller know you are buying a lot of items. I usually wait until I have everything I want set aside. Then I will ask the owner what he or she wants for everything.

Sometimes owners will go through each and every piece giving a price for each or sometimes they will just give a quick look and name a price for everything. If an owner offers a great deal, go for it. But if the offer is a little high, ask for a small percentage off the price. If the price is a lot higher than you expected, ask the seller what item is driving up the cost and consider not buying that piece or negotiating it separately.

TIMING IS EVERYTHING

There are many great books that will teach you the art of negotiation, and if you are inexperienced, we would recommend you read some of the top sellers on the subject. However, there is no substitution for practice and experience. You must get out there and start negotiating for the items you want to buy. Sometimes, a person with whom you are trying to negotiate with will say no. But most people will say yes or at least be willing to negotiate. Unrealistic sellers are the ones who usually refuse to negotiate the price. If you run into these sellers in the early part of the day, come back late in the day. They have usually received a dose of reality by then and are more willing to work with someone on the price. This strategy works well especially at yard sales, flea markets, and tag sales.

If sellers have some great items, do not to insult or upset them if they refuse to negotiate early in the day. After all, they have the whole day to try to sell the item to other customers at full price. Be polite when you refuse to pay their asking price. You do not want them to have bad feelings about you when you come back later in the day. Daren and I have been to many yard and tag sales that have had a lot of great merchandise left at the final hours of the sale. This is the best time to negotiate a good deal. Sellers know they only have a few hours left to move their merchandise, and if the merchandise does not sell they will have to do something else with it. After yard sales, owners will likely donate the unsold items, receiving nothing but a tax receipt for the goods. Flea market owners will have to pack up, move, and store the unsold items until the next sale. After a tag sale, the person running the sale may have to return all unsold merchandise to the owners or estates and therefore will receive no commission. So it is in the sellers' best interest to negotiate the price.

The more negotiations you engage in, the more you will be able to hone your skill. The important point is that almost every buying situation can and should involve negotiation. We want to teach you to think of creative ways to negotiate and to identify situations where negotiations will benefit you.

NEGOTIATION BASICS

1. Be willing to walk away from a deal. Never feel forced to complete a transaction if you are not getting a great price. There is always another deal waiting to be found. Sometimes walking away will make the seller lower his price.

2. Do not be afraid of silence. It is normal for silence to be uncomfortable in a negotiation situation. Let silence work for you. If the price is too high, let the buyer know it is too high and then say nothing. Sometimes it is better not to say anything so the pressure to speak and change the price is on the seller.

3. Ask the seller questions about the item before price is discussed. Many times the seller will provide information that will affect the value of the piece. The owner may point out a flaw you did not see or tell you that the item has been repaired. The owner may be able to give some history on the piece that will enable you to sell it better in the future. Unless you know the seller, though, be cautious about his or her opinion on the value and history of a piece.

4. If there is minor damage on the item, be sure to point it out to the seller. A seller may have been unaware of the damage and may reduce the price accordingly. If you find major damage on an item, you should consider carefully before purchasing it at any price. Condition is a huge factor in resale.

5. Do not let your emotions dictate your purchase price. This happens a great deal at auctions. A lot of people get "auction fever" and keep bidding past the point of value. Auction fever is good for the auctioneer but never for the buyer. Your mantra should be *there is always more.*

Chapter Nine
Ethics

ETHICS WHEN BUYING TO RESELL

People often ask me if I feel guilty buying items for so little and selling them for so much. The answer is always no but with an explanation. There is a great deal of work that goes into buying to resell and a certain amount of risk taking, but there is also a code of ethics in this business.

When I have been hired as a professional appraiser, I never purchase the items I am appraising. To do that would be against the professional code and definitely in violation of my business and personal ethics. If a person has received an appraisal from me on an item, I can sell that item for them online or in another auction format, but I cannot buy it outright. The difference is that when I am buying goods for resale, I want to get those goods at the lowest price possible so I can return the highest profit possible. When I buy items for resale, I am assuming the risk that I may not be able to resell these goods for more money than I paid for them. So the less I paid for goods, the more likely I am to make a profit. The owner of those goods wants to get the most they can for their items, so the owner and I would be in adversarial positions. It would be unethical for me to appraise an item and then try to purchase that item.

When I am the consignor of goods, the owner of the goods and I are on the same side. We have the same goal, which is to sell those goods to a third party for the highest price possible. I receive a commission based on the sale price of the goods, therefore, we *both* want the goods to sell high. Also, when I sell goods on consignment, the transaction is in a public forum, such as eBay, where all is transparent to every party involved. When I am selling items as a consignor for others, I give the owner of the goods a true and honest representation of what I believe the item will sell for online. Auctions are unpredictable by their very natures, but I can usually predict the sale price within 20 percent.

An Almost Wallace Grande Rip-off

We received a call from an elderly gentleman whose wife had passed away several months earlier. He wanted to sell some of their possessions so he could downsize into a smaller home. One of the items he showed to us was a set of sterling silver flatware. The set was a service for twelve of Wallace Grande Baroque, which included many serving pieces. He said he had been offered $300 by an antiques dealer and asked us if we thought he should take the offer. I told him that I could get ten times that amount for the silver online. I sold the set of sterling flatware for him for over $3,500. We both were happy that he decided to consign the silver with me instead of selling it outright to the antiques dealer.

It was obvious to anyone that this man knew very little about his wife's sterling flatware, and he could easily have been taken advantage of. I am equally sure that the antiques dealer knew that the silver was worth at least ten times what he'd offered. I think the dealer was unethical. At the very least, he should have offered the gentleman a third or half the resale value of the item. I believe this dealer saw an opportunity to take advantage of an elderly person who was grieving. Luckily, the man was sharper than the dealer and sought out a second opinion before he sold the sterling.

When I am acting as my own agent seeking out bargains to resell, I do not feel an obligation to give a free appraisal of an item before I purchase it. It should also be said that we, of course, could not and do not try to force anyone to sell something to us they do not want to sell. Most of the time, we pay what or close to what the person is asking for the item. If they happen to be asking too little, it is not up to me to point that out to them. You would not go into a department store and offer to pay more than what the price tag reads.

A Keyboard Not Worth the Hassle

One day Daren and I saw a yard sale in progress and decided to stop. Daren spotted a very expensive piano keyboard, for which the woman was asking an extremely undervalue price. It was a large item, and we did not want to hassle with the shipping, so Daren told the lady the price she was asking was very low. He told her that she could get three or four times that amount by selling it online. She stated that she knew it was an expensive keyboard, but she wanted to get rid of it. I told her she could take it to an eBay drop-off store and they would sell it for her on consignment. She said she was too busy and would rather just sell it at the yard sale for a few dollars. The point of this story is that sometimes people do not care if they are selling their items for less than the market value. Their only focus is to get rid of the items.

Whenever we purchase an item, we spend a good deal of time and money in the process of reselling the piece. We have to photograph and write up a listing for the item. We have to pay the eBay and PayPal fees when the item sells. We also have to pack up the item and pay for shipping supplies. So we add value to the item by all the work involved in selling the piece. If the original owner wanted to get top dollar for the item, he or she could list it on eBay instead of having a yard sale, but most people do not want to go to the time and trouble that would require.

The lines between appraising, consignment, and buying are very clear and defined and must remain so if we are to maintain a good reputation. I personally believe that it is wrong to take advantage of a person who, for whatever reason, is not able to make an informed decision to sell. I have come across people who are selling items that belonged to a deceased loved one while they are still deep in the grieving stage or elderly people who no longer have the ability to barter for a fair price. In these cases, your personal ethics will need to guide you. When faced with situations like those, I always take the high road. I either offer a price that is more than fair or offer to sell the item for the person so he or she can receive the highest possible price. I always say that no bargain is worth ruining my reputation as an honest person. I have to be able to lay my head down on my pillow each night and sleep peacefully. No bargain is worth more than that.

ONLINE BUYING AND SELLING ETHICS

Earlier, I wrote about buyers making up complaints about an item to get a reduced price. I would like to revisit that from a different perspective in this chapter—that of the buyer. First, the practice is dishonest, and second, it makes it hard for people with legitimate complaints to receive fair treatment by sellers. You should not expect items that are vintage or antique to be perfect. Any major damage like chips, stains, or repairs should be listed, but do not expect the seller to have gone over the piece with a jeweler's loop. If a reasonable third party would believe that you received a fair deal and that the piece was properly listed, do not try to receive a partial refund. I mention a reasonable third party, because some people are extremely critical when it comes to their collectibles. I have had buyers start out their emails with the phrase, "I know I am being very picky but ..." If you feel **you should** start out your email with that phrase, stop yourself from continuing **and do not** send it.

However, if a **piece has** damage or significant issues, then you certainly have a right to complain, **and you** should be able to return the goods. Also, if the seller listed an item as new **and you** can see that it has been worn or used, then I believe you have a legitimate reason to complain. Always try to take the high road, and remember that sellers are human and will make honest mistakes. Do not automatically assume the seller is dishonest or trying to take advantage of you. There are fraudulent eBayers, but they will take your money, and you will receive nothing in return. It is very unlikely that a seller who has been selling on eBay for years and who has good feedback will intentionally try to deceive. Any seller who has some experience knows that even a little deception is not worth the trouble it causes down the line.

Returning to the perspective of the seller, when you are selling online, take the time to examine the piece so you can list any and all damage you can find. Use your eyes, but also use your hands. It is sometimes easier to find a chip or damage with your fingers, especially on pottery and glass. For beginners, it is natural to want to make your item sound as good as possible. It is tempting to "gild the lily" and to minimize any damage or issues. Do not be tempted into this trap. It will be a losing situation for both you and the buyer. You may get a few more bids, but making your item sound better than it is will not be worth the resulting hassle. When the buyer gets the piece, he or she will be disappointed and the piece will be returned to you and/or you will receive negative feedback. Once an item is sold, the last thing you want is for it to come back to you. It is very costly and time consuming to have an item shipped back and have to re-list and reship it all over again. Be honest to a fault on all your goods.

Another good reason to examine your items closely is so that you will know if a buyer's complaint is legitimate or not. If the buyer's complaint is legitimate, and you made an honest mistake, then try to make up for the mistake in a way that will please your buyer. However, if you feel the complaint is not legitimate then question the buyer and ask for pictures. Sometimes items are damaged during shipment, and other times the buyer is trying to negotiate the price after the sale. I rarely give partial refunds and never give them in response to threats of negative feedback. If I am suspicious of the buyer's claim, but he or she is insistent, I demand that the buyer return the item for a refund. If I let a buyer keep the goods at a discounted price, it is not fair to the other bidders, to me, or to my consignment customers.

Chapter Ten
Trends, Styles, and Terminology You Need to Know

KEEP PACE WITH THE MARKET

In this business, keeping current with what is selling well is extremely important. Depending on what area you plan to focus on, the trends can move very quickly or more slowly. As we have said before, anything related to technology will change rapidly, so you should always move those types of goods in and out of your inventory quickly. Fashion is another area that tends to move quickly. Last year's fashions may be a great bargain at the outlet malls, but clothing is only worth buying if the style is something classic, not something that was last year's fad.

Other markets tend to move up or down in a slower pace. Trends in the antiques and collectibles markets can and do move in and out of popularity, but most of the time the movement is slow. People who collect Danish Modern items are not going to suddenly decide the Modern look is out of fashion and convert to the Victorian style in one season. A style or look can sometimes get "hot" very quickly, but it usually takes years before its popularity will start to wane, and then the price will slowly start to drop.

But the antiques and collectibles markets also have subtle nuances that make huge differences in prices. One Weller vase may command a price of $8,000 while another of the same size with a similar shape may only receive $3,000 in the open market. The difference can depend on a number of things. It could be that one style is more popular with buyers or it could be that the more expensive vase was made in limited numbers and thus is rare.

Know Styles and Historical Periods

If you plan to sell antiques and collectibles, it is important to educate yourself on the historical styles and artistic and architectural movements. *It is imperative when listing items online to be able to correctly identify the style in order to attract the right bidders to the auction.*

Everyone has read or heard stories about rare and extremely valuable items purchased at flea markets and yard sales. That could happen, but you are more likely to find great items that are valuable but not rare. For example, while it is unlikely that you will find any furniture or items from the Rococo period (1650–1790), you most certainly will find reproductions made in that *style*. And you will likely find great pieces from the later periods such as Art Nouveau (1890–1905) and Art Deco (1925–1935), which are affordable and definitely worth collecting and selling.

We are also going to include some styles that are not historical period references but terminology used to describe the style of an item. For example, southwestern style refers to the look of an object, but it has no historical reference. Rather it was named for the area where the style first became popular and where many items in that style were originally made.

Below we have listed the major historical styles, popular terminology, and some key characteristics to help you spot them. Keep in mind that many of the styles overlap and have the same qualities, as one period transitioned into another. In one porcelain figurine you may see both the curved lines of Art Nouveau and the angles of Art Deco. There are hundreds of books and websites to help guide you further in the learning process. Many of the books and websites have photographic examples of objects and artwork that can better demonstrate the look of the style.

Historical Periods

Classical Greek and Roman

The classical Greek style usually features one or more of three basic orders: Doric, Ionic, or Corinthian. The Doric order was the most plain of the three orders featuring simple square or rounded columns. The Ionic columns were fluted with spiral scrolls and sometimes had added decoration of acanthus leaves. The third order was Corinthian, which was more ornate but also more delicate in it columns and design.

The Roman architecture borrowed much from the classical Greek style, but Roman architects added the wonderful invention of the dome and vault. The Romans used a primitive form of concrete and developed a highly organized water system, which channeled water that was flowing down from a mountain into an elaborate duct system throughout Rome. This water was a primitive plumbing system that flowed to the public bath houses and the private homes of the very wealthy.

The classic Greek sculpture is familiar to many of us. These statues usually depict people in action—enjoying sporting, bathing, or other activities. Freedom of movement and artistic expression can be seen in the classic sculptures. Often the statues show incredible detail of the human body in little or no clothing. When dressed, the Greek and Roman figures were clothed similarly. The dress consisted mainly of tunics and togas or other loose clothing.

Many of the classic Greek and Roman statues are being reproduced today in resin. The resin statues are very inexpensive versions of marble and bronze statues.

Baroque Period (1600–1700 AD)

The Baroque style was a French-based look. It is full of geometrical shapes, heavy patterns, and ornamentation. The style is very dramatic and extravagant, so much so that it often overwhelms the viewer. Baroque architecture was large and elaborate with curved and broken lines. The buildings were expansive with the focus on heavy decoration and opulence.

The sculptures and paintings of the Baroque period are very emotionally engaging for the viewer. Drama and energy are displayed in exaggerated and complicated scenes of heroic battles or religious figures. The Baroque style gives the eye very little room to rest, but it is very compelling to view. For the greatest example of the Baroque period, look to the Palace of Versailles built by Louis XIV, king of France from 1644–1715.

Rococo Period (1650–1790 AD)

The Rococo period, which was also started in France, overlapped the Baroque period, and the two had many elements in common, such as overabundance and emphasis on heavy decoration. However, the Rococo style was much more graceful and focused on the lighter side of life, including romance and nature. The term Rococo came from the French words *rocaille*, which means rock, and *coquille*, meaning shell.

You will see many shells and rocks as well as other natural elements in the art and sculptures of the Rococo period. Scenes of the Rococo period feature light or frivolous activities set in idyllic gardens or mythological places. The feeling of the art is relaxed, sensual, and playful. In it, the human and animal forms blend together with nature.

Early American Colonial Period (1640–1780 AD)

The Early American or American Colonial style was the complete opposite of the Baroque style. When the colonists came to America, they brought with them many of their European styles and traditions, but they were most heavily influenced by English styles. In the United States, the look was more conservative and less ornate than the English styles of William and Mary, Queen Ann, and Georgian styles.

The Colonial style was simple and straightforward without a lot of embellishment. The architectural style included pitched roofs with central entryways and evenly spaced, shuttered windows, which sat directly beneath the roofline. The furniture was simple, rustic, and functional with clean straight lines. Ceramics were popular at the time, but they too were simple with earthy colors. The art was in the realist style. It featured nature, farms, and rural scenes. Portraits were also popular, and some artists traveled from town to town painting portraits of the people who could afford such extravagances.

Needlework and quilting were extremely popular art forms among the early settlers.

Federal Period (1780–1820 AD)

The Federal period was a graceful transition from the Colonial period. The Federal-style furniture combined the neoclassic characteristics of Hepplewhite and Sheraton. The look was characterized by light, feminine, graceful construction with straight lines and tapered legs. The use of inlay, contrasting veneers, and exotic woods was common.

Georgian Period (1720–1830 AD)

This period was named for the rulers of England, George I–IV. The Georgian style was a throwback to the classic elements of the Greeks and Romans. It had understated elegance, rigid lines, and was heavily influence by Palladianism. Palladianism is a design style created by sixteenth century architect Andreas Palladio. Chippendale and Hepplewhite furniture was popular during this period.

Decorative object adhered to the clean, light style of the period. Most of the silver had straight, classic lines with a simple etched or embossed design or a little flourish on the tip.

There was a slight Oriental influence, which can be seen in the small details such as the fan-shaped designs above the doors and window and in the decorative items in the Georgian homes.

Victorian Period (1840–1900 AD)

The Victorian style is known today as one that is lavish and ornate. The upper middle class home of the time would have been full of bric-a-brac; overstuffed sofas; and dark, heavy curtains. During this period of history, the middle and upper middle classes grew, and people wanted to show off their newfound wealth. Socializing was important to the Victorians, and people attended or held parties several nights a week. The Victorians were responsible for expanding the number of dinner serving pieces so that every possible food item had a special utensil with which it was served. The flatware and china was decorated with ribbons, bows, and flowers. The style was often considered feminine because it had a romantic look. The colors of this period were dark and rich with a mixture of floral and other patterns.

Many of the homes of this period were referred to as "gingerbread" houses due to the lavish trim that adorned the outside of the homes. The key words that describe the Victorian style are busy, ornate, and overdone. Other terms associated with the Victorian Period are Queen Anne and the Aesthetic movement.

Edwardian Period (1901–1910)

This style is named for King Edward VII of England, who reigned from 1901–1910 after the death of Queen Victoria. The Edwardian style came from the need for a change from the clutter and heaviness of the Victorian era. This new style was lighter and cleaner with an emphasis on the elegant but simple. This style was somewhat eclectic, with influences from the Arts and Crafts movement, Art Nouveau, and Queen Anne Style.

Arts and Crafts Period (1860–1900)

The Arts and Crafts period is often referred to as a "movement," because it was a rebellion against the forces of industrialization in England. In this time period, many decorative items were, for the first time, being mass-produced and as a result had inferior quality. What this movement hoped to bring back to life was the respect of and desire for quality handmade goods. William Morris set up his own company with fellow artists, which produced everything from jewelry to furniture. The look was simple with little ornamentation, and the goods were handmade and of high quality.

The Arts and Crafts style focused on the beauty of natural materials and earthy, subtle colors. Many of the metalwork pieces were made of hand-hammered silver, copper, and pewter. Look to the manufacturers Carl Sorensen and Roycroft to find excellent examples of the Arts and Crafts style in metals. Pottery made during this time was also simple but well made. Many of the pieces had bulbous shapes with simple, rounded handles or straight-angled handles.

The colors were often matte colors of nature such as robin's egg blue and soft greens and browns. Look to pottery makers such as Rookwood, Fulper, and Grueby for classic examples of the Arts and Crafts style. Also see the section on the Mission style for additional information.

Art Nouveau Period (1890–1905)

Art Nouveau was known as the "new style" or "art of nature." The Art Nouveau style was reflected in objects that had asymmetrical shapes, flowing lines, arches, and swirling, plant-like designs. Flowers and vines embellished, entwined, and encircled all the art forms from this period in a gentle, soft form. The furniture of this period was generally made of mahogany or walnut and occasionally burl wood. Soft curves and inlays of darker woods accented many of the pieces.

The female form was the center of the Art Nouveau art, ceramics, and sculptures. She was displayed as a soft, slightly rounded, sensual maiden with long flowing ribbons of hair, which was sometimes adorned with flowers or vines. She was almost always nude or partially nude with loosely hanging, draping clothing. Many of the decorative pieces were set in nature or had nature-related themes. Dancing and bathing were also popular themes. Study the sculptures of Raoul

Francois Larche, Louis Chalon, and Carl Kauba for classic Art Nouveau at its best.

The art from this period had many of the same themes as the decorative objects such as the flowing lines and natural settings. Poster art had become very common during this period, and some period poster art can still be found at reasonable prices. You will also find great examples of Art Nouveau art in the reproduction prints that are widely available today. Study the art of Maxfield Parrish, Gustav Klimt, and Alphonse Mucha to learn the style of Art Nouveau.

The Art Nouveau period was a time of experimentation for potters in Europe and the United States. Potters felt free to try new and unusual shapes, glazes, and motifs. The general themes were still nature and sensual maidens, but working with clay and color enabled the potters to bring unique looks to life. Most of the European factories produced lovely examples of Art Nouveau. Look to Moorcroft, Royal Dux, and Amphora Ware by Reissner, Stellmacher, and Kessel. Good examples can be found by American manufactures including Weller, Roseville, and Rookwood.

Art glass was at its peak during the Art Nouveau period. Glass makers such as Tiffany, Loetz, and Galle are well-known for their incredible glass productions from this era. This style again showcases nature with lovely interpretations of flowers, plants, and insects. Look for handmade pieces with flowing lines, detailed workmanship, and stunning colors. Many glassmakers used metals such as silver and bronze in overlays to add movement and drama to the pieces. Other great glassmakers from this period are Quezal, Steuben, and Lalique.

Jewelry is another area where you can find amazing pieces of period Art Nouveau. Many jewelry makers of this time used inexpensive materials but incredible craftsmanship to produce lovely jewelry items. To find great examples, look at the works of Tiffany, Lalique, and Unger Brothers. Much of the jewelry from this period was not signed, so let the quality of the work guide you, not just the name on the back.

Art Deco Period (1925–1935 AD)

Where Art Nouveau was flowing and curvy, Art Deco featured clean, straight lines and angles. Embracing the emerging industrial age, Art Deco images often included stylized airplanes, cars, ships, and skyscrapers. The stair step profile was everywhere in the Art Deco designs, as were many geographical shapes, zigzags, and lightning bolts.

Two other influences on the Art Deco style were the film industry and the discovery of King Tut's Tomb. The film industry burst into full bloom during the Art Deco period and was very popular with the masses. The first "talkie" film, *The Jazz Singer*, made its debut in 1927. Rich satins, silks, and furs where mixed with highly polished wood and lacquer furniture. Chrome and mirrors were also very popular in the decorative items. Think about the old-time movie stars like Greta Garbo and Marlene Dietrich, and you will get the feel for Art Deco.

With the exciting discovery of King Tut's Tomb in 1922, an Egyptian influence soon found its way into many of the pieces from the 1920s and '30s. The tomb's discovery was major news during the time, and as more and more artifacts were brought into public view, the fascination with Egypt grew.

The women featured in Art Deco pieces sometimes had an Egyptian look to them with dark makeup and upper arm bracelets. The flapper girl was also prominent in many pieces; with chin-length cropped or bobbed hair, she was usually thinner and more angular than her predecessor. The Deco girl appeared carefree and jovial and was often surrounded by geometrical shapes. One of the most popular themes in lighting was the Deco girl holding a glass sphere, which acted as the globe of the lamp.

The furniture was strong with streamline shapes and more masculine than the Nouveau furniture. The fabrics and rugs had geometrical designs and patterns. For excellent examples of Art Deco glass, look to Lalique, Daum, and Tiffany. For pottery and china, look to Susie Cooper, Clarice Cliff, and Doulton & Co.

Mid-Century/Danish Modern (1950s–1970s)

The cool, sleek sophisticated lines of the Mid-Century Modern look dates back to the late 1950s and are still popular today. The outstanding designer Charles Eames' name is synonymous with this period, which is sometimes referred to as "Eames Era."

This modern approach to furniture and style stressed function and simplicity of design. Famous sculptor Horatio Greenough made famous the quote "form follows function," which means that the function of the items should be the most important aspect of any item. The great architects and designers of this look were Charles and Ray Eames, Frank Lloyd Wright, and Louis Isadore Kahn.

The Mid-Century Modern look was simple and free of ornamentation or unnecessary detail. In the Modern home, there were no shelves holding hundreds of little bric-a-brac items or lacy curtains. Rather, there was a lovely but limited collection of pottery or glass with simple lines. The colors were earthy and calm, and the feel was cool and clean. The geometric forms were present in fabric, but solid colors dominated this style. The bold patterns and shapes were saved for accent pillows and decorative pieces.

The Mid-Century Modern look was not all serious and strictly functional. Many of the items such as lighting, pottery, and art had a fun and funky twist. Some of the art was abstract or surreal, but other pieces looked similar in style to a comic book. See the works of Pablo Picasso, Roy Lichtenstein, and Andy Warhol.

The glass and pottery of this period was often asymmetrical with little or no adornment. Again, clean, simple lines were a key element to this style, but that does not mean the pieces lacked beauty. Lovely glazes and shapes were highlighted by the lack of frill and garnish.

For quality examples of Mid-Century Modern decorative items look to the works of Verner Panton and Charles Eames. For glass examples look to Murano Glass and Blenko. For classic examples in pottery look to Russell Wright, Upsala Ekeby, and select pieces by Rosenthal.

To learn more about the Mid-Century Modern style, look to other terms such as Pop Art, Abstract Art, and Contemporary style.

These are examples of classical Greek statues. Some of these statues are made from marble and others are made from inexpensive resin.

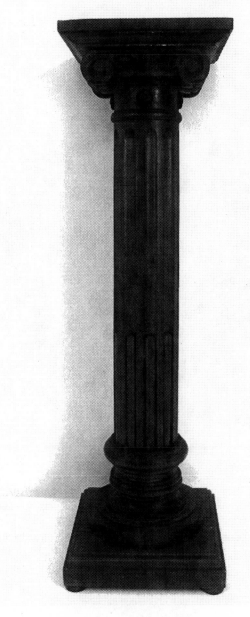

This is an example of a classical Greek ionic column.

This is an antique, sterling silver sash holder from the Rococo Revival Period.

This is a federal-style double fern stand with its original green paint and brass castors. Note the simplistic, functional design.

This card table is a nice quality reproduction in the federal style. Note the narrow legs and simple inlay.

This is a Chippendale-style, drop front desk made in Philadelphia in the late 1880s.

This collection represents the Arts and Crafts style. The two silver bowls are hand-hammered. The pottery pieces have a simple, earthy-colored glaze.

This silver-plated tea set by Barbour Silver Company dates to the Victorian period. Note the ornate hand-chased decoration on the pieces.

These are examples of furniture from the Victorian period. Although not as ornate as many Victorian pieces, they still reflect the style of the times. Furniture with needlepoint cushions, such as this stool, was very popular.

This picture represents items from the Victorian Era. The large, oval frame has a gesso treatment, which is applied plaster of Paris that has then been painted to simulate striped wood grain. This was common in both the Victorian and Edwardian periods.

This grouping represents the Art Nouveau period. Art Nouveau style is
known for its soft line and nature themes.

The print by Alphonse Mucha perfectly reflects the Art Nouveau woman. She is soft and sensuous, dressed in a flowing gown, and surrounded by nature. Also represented here is an Art Nouveau light and silver pedestal.

These are two modern reproductions of nineteenth century majolica.
Both pieces are made in high relief with natural themes. The pedestal
has an Asian influence.

This grouping represents the Art Deco period. Note the sharper lines and geometric forms. The lamp to the left is from the 1939 New York World's Fair.

This collection represents the Modern and Danish Modern designs. Note the clean lines and lack of embellishment.

These different styles of jewelry are, from top center clockwise: an Arts & Crafts sterling silver bracelet; a collection of Modern-style jewelry; a collection of Art Nouveau jewelry; a collection of Art Deco jewelry; and a collection of Victorian jewelry.

OTHER STYLE TERMS

Gothic

The Gothic style originated in France in the middle of the twelfth century and has had a series of revivals in Europe and America in the eighteenth, nineteenth, and twentieth centuries. The style is characterized by the use of pointed arches, ornamental gables, flying buttresses, and foils.

French Provincial Style (Late 1600s)

The French Provincial style began under the rule of Louis XIV in the late 1600s. This style was formal but much less ornate than the Baroque style of Versailles. This style was popular in rural homes and chateaus of the French nobles and had revivals of popularity in the 1920s and 1960s. French Provincial was elegant with an emphasis on balance and symmetry. Many refer to the French Provincial style as French Country.

Louis XIV Style (1644–1715)

The Louis XIV style is another name for the Baroque style. Louis XIV was dubbed both Sun King and Builder of Versailles. His palace was richly and ornately decorated with paintings on the walls and ceiling frescos. Statues, fountains, and figurines covered in lavish gilt filled every room, and no detail was forgotten.

Queen Anne Style (1702–1714)

Although Queen Anne ruled England in the early 1700s, the style named after her did not materialize until the rule of Queen Victoria and the Victorian period. The Queen Anne style was mainly seen in architecture and furniture.

Queen Anne furniture was light and graceful with simple lines that emphasized the curvilinear. The shell motif was an important element of the Queen Anne style. This shell is often thought to be a fan or sunburst, but, looking closely, you will see a shell shape. Another element that was prominent in Queen Anne furniture was the cabriole leg. A cabriole leg is described as having a bent knee and then an incurved ankle going down to a simple pad foot.

Empire Style (1800–1830)

The Empire Style took its name from Napoleon Bonaparte's rule of France, which was known as the First Empire. French designers were sponsored by the French government to create a style that was to glorify Napoleon and his rule. The designers went back to ancient Greece and Rome for design elements. The Empire style took hold in Italy, Imperial Russia, and other European cities before and after the fall of Napoleon.

The furniture was made of dark, heavy wood with simple rectangle designs and a few decorative details of palm leaves or sphinxes to commemorate Napoleon's successful campaign in Egypt. Examples of the furniture include pedestal tables with paw or claw feet and sleigh beds. Other decorative motifs included acanthus leaves, lyre, rosettes, dolphins, and the eagle.

Aesthetic Movement (1868–1901)

The Aesthetic movement began in the late nineteenth century at the end of the Victorian period. This movement was fueled by the phrase "art for art's sake," coined by philosopher Victor Cousin. This movement believed that art did not have to have a function or purpose but only had to be beautiful. Famous names associated with this movement are Oscar Wilde, John Keats, and Percy Bysshe Shelley.

Eastlake Style (1870–1900 AD)

The Eastlake period began toward the end of the Victorian period and was named after the designer who inspired it—Charles Eastlake. The term Eastlake is usually used in reference to a home's architecture or furniture and other small pieces such as bookshelves and cabinets. Eastlake used simple, rectilinear construction with basic geometric design. Most of his furniture was made of walnut, mahogany, or cherry, and it featured parallel carved grooves, serrated edges, chip carving, and some inlaid details.

Majolica Maiolica

The first examples of tin-glazed earthenware date back to the ninth century in the Middle East. By the eleventh century, this earthenware was imported to Italy and Spain, and soon those countries began to make their own versions of the ceramics.

During the Renaissance, the Italian potters began to elevate their craft, creating more beautiful and elaborate pieces of this earthenware.

However, the term Majolica is most frequently used to describe nineteenth-century, lead-glazed, high-relief ceramics made in Europe. This pottery almost always had a natural theme featuring plants, insects, animals, and water. This type of Majolica usually had a great deal of detail and was very colorful. You will find a soup tureen shaped like a cabbage or a pedestal that looks like an old log. This look would be considered a subset of the Art Nouveau period. Look to the works of Hugo Lonitz, Minton, and Capodimonte.

Mission Style (early twentieth-century America)

The mission style drew its inspiration and designs from the Spanish missions of California. The homes and public structures in this style had massive walls with thick, heavy exposed beams in the ceilings. The outside of the structures were made of stucco, plaster, or adobe bricks.

The furniture style is easily recognizable by its dark stained wood with rectangular shapes and open planks of wood on the sides. Most of the Mission pieces had little to no decoration, but sometimes there was a slight carving or simple inlay. The most famous manufacturers of mission furniture are the Stickley Brothers.

Southwest Style

The name was derived from the place where the look originated. The Southwestern style took its inspiration from the animals, people, and places found in southwest United States. The main colors are those found in nature in those areas, such as the red of the clay, yellow of the sand, and the clear blue of the open sky. This style was influenced by the handmade crafts of the Native American Indian, such as rugs, pottery, and jewelry. Some of the motifs were lizards, cacti, and snakes.

Chapter Eleven
Sourcing: Places to Find and Sell Your Goods

RETAIL PURCHASING

Purchasing from a retail store to sell online sounds like a losing proposition, but it does not have to be. If you find the right situation, you can make money when you buy retail and resell. Unless you have your own retail store, there is really no proper way to sell retail; so selling will not be covered in the retail section, but the other sections will cover both selling and buying.

Daren found a coupon to be used at the online Disney store, so he searched the store's website for a great deal. He found they had the Master Replicas Nautilus *Twenty Thousand Leagues under the Sea* ships on sale, and Disney was offering free shipping. This ship normally sold for $499.99, but with his extra coupon and the sales price, Daren was able to purchase the ship for $130. He looked on eBay and found that the ships were selling under the Buy-it-Now option for $299.99. So to under-price the competition on eBay, Daren listed his ship for $290, and it sold right away. He made a profit of $160, and all we had to do was slap another shipping label on the box and send it on its way.

Daren only had one coupon so he could not get the same exact deal on another ship, but the Disney store was still offering the ships at $199.99 with free shipping. He knew we could sell the ships for $290 quickly on eBay, so he purchased two more. He only made $90 each on the next two ships, but it was still not a bad profit for such little work. He sold a total of five ships while Disney was offering the free shipping. So far he had made $520 in this quick resale adventure.

Daren went online to the Disney Store and found the Nautilus was no longer available. He called the customer service line and found there were only a few ships left in stock, so Disney had removed the Nautilus from the website. However, they were still offering the item to phone-in customers who specifically asked for the ship. Daren purchased two more. At this time, it was only two months until Christmas, so we decided to hold onto out last two ships until Christmas was a little closer. When the Disney online store removed the Master Replica Nautilus from the website, the sale price on eBay soared. In just a matter of a few weeks, the Buy-it-Now price went from $299 to $350. A few weeks later, the price was averaging $400. After Thanksgiving, the price of the ship went to $450, so we decided it was time to cash in on our purchases. We sold the last two Nautilus ships for $450 each.

This is not only a good example of retail purchasing for resale, but we also should point out that you should shop around and make sure you are getting the best price before you buy. If the people who purchased the Nautilus ship from us on eBay would have gone to the Disney store online, they would have gotten a much better deal.

Before you rush out and begin to purchase online Disney items, remember that the vast majority of Disney items resell for much lower than the retail price. This example worked, because the Nautilus ship is an expensive, limited item that is highly desired by collectors. These transactions were also helped by the fact that the limited supply was exhausted when we were trying to sell our ships, and Christmas was less than two months away when we began. All these factors together made for a great chance to resell a classic Disney collectible.

This is a new, in the Box Nautilus Master Replicas *Twenty Thousand Leagues Under the Sea* ship by Disney.

Musical instruments can be great item to buy for resale and are readily available on the secondhand market.

GOING-OUT-OF-BUSINESS SALES OR LIQUIDATIONS

There are several ways you can buy at retail or retail-like stores and still resell the items at a profit. You can look for stores that are going out of business and are selling their merchandise at hugely discounted prices. These have to be true going-out-of-business sales. There are many companies that professionally go "out of business" all year long. I have seen stores mark the prices up 250 percent then slash them to "80 percent off," trying to trick consumers into believing they are getting huge discounts. Many times prices are outrageously high. Prices at the "out of business" store can sometimes be two or three times more than those at a regular, full-price store. Do not be fooled. Shop around, and know the true retail price of an item before you buy it. What you are looking for is a small retail store that is going out of business.

FACTORY OUTLETS

This can be a great place to get bargains if the factory outlet is a true factory outlet store. There are sellers on eBay whose entire business is based on the clothes purchased at factory outlets. There are factory outlet malls all across the country that charge the same price as the retail store or offer lower quality merchandise. There are some manufacturers who make clothing lines specifically to sell at factory outlets. The material or manufacturer process may be of a lesser quality. Most labels will show that the item was made for the factory outlet. There are also many "seconds," irregulars, and damaged goods at outlet malls. This is not what you want unless the store is having a huge closeout wale with at extremely low prices.

What you want to find are true first-quality merchandise offered at extreme discounts. Most of the items you find at the outlets will be last season's unsold items or discontinued merchandise.

In Arlington, Texas, there is a store called Discount Dillard's. This store sells last season's merchandise from all the Dillard's department stores in the region for 75 percent or more off the retail price. Whenever we visit my parents in Texas, we go to the store to purchase clothing for our family and for resale. We will buy $300–$500 worth of designer clothing and hold it until the appropriate season before listing it online.

The last time we went to the Discount Dillard's was June, and most of the clothing was from the fall and winter season. The store was offering an additional 10 percent off men's clothing, which was 85 percent off the retail price. Due to the extra incentive, we decided to invest in just men's clothing, and we purchased $300 worth of long sleeve shirts by such designers as Ralph Lauren, Calvin Klein, and Nautica. We made sure we purchased popular name brands and styles that would appeal to the broadest range of buyers. As you might expect, the vast majority of clothing was not popular in the retail store, which is why it was at the discount Dillard's store. If you look long enough, you will find many very quality pieces that will sell nicely online.

We held these shirts until the fall, when men are looking to buy long sleeve shirts. We could have held them until the Christmas buying season in December since they would be perfect gifts, but we already had so much scheduled for that time period that we decided to sell the shirts in late fall. We could have listed the items as soon as we came home, but they would have sold for a lot less, because it was in the middle of summer and very few people think about long-sleeved shirts and sweaters in July. *Buy in the off season, and sell in the in season.*

There are people who are employed in the retail sector who purchase goods using their employee discount. Usually they wait for a good sale, and when they add their 20 percent or more employee discount, they can get the goods at a very nice price. Since they work at the stores, they will also have first pick of the quality merchandise just after it goes on sale before the general public. Some companies now are forbidding their employees from selling company merchandise online.

The final retail example we will give is purchasing "hot" items for resale. I am sure everyone has heard of hot toys or electronic games that sell for three or four times the retail price online. This usually occurs every Christmas, but there are times when supply catches up with demand, and the reseller gets stuck with the merchandise. Be careful when trying to play the odds on what will be hot each Christmas. Sometimes what the experts predict will be a hot toy turns out to be a dud with consumers.

THE AUCTION

The first record of auctions extends back to 500 BC when young women were sold as wives by their fathers or owners. Bidding for the most beautiful maidens was vigorous, but the fathers of unattractive women often had to add dowries in order to get a bid on their daughters.

In the Roman Empire, auctions were started with a spear being driven into the ground, which is much more dramatic than the rap of an auction gavel that is used today. The Roman auctions were used to sell the massive amounts of war plunder brought back from conquered enemies, but it was also used to sell family estate items. A Roman family's items could be sold at auction at their discretion or by force to pay the family's debt. Not much has changed in two thousand years.

When the pilgrims arrived in America, they brought the tradition of auctioneering with them from Europe. The American auction was used for everything, including real estate, crops, and especially furs. The fur trade was a major factor in the new America's development and settlement. But it wasn't until the Civil War that auctioneers became known as, or were given the title of, colonels. During and after the Civil War, officers with the rank of colonel or above could auction off seized assets and war surplus. These colonels would travel from one area to the next taking property and holding public auctions. At this time, nonmilitary auctioneers began to dress much like their military counterparts and travel the same areas auctioning off goods. This practice was so common that the general public began to recognize all auctioneers as colonels.

The Great Depression was a hard time for auctioneers, as it was for many others. Most of their business came from selling off family farms and assets.

Today the modern auction is nothing like its predecessor. Technology has stepped in and made the modern day auction house better, faster, and more accurate. The auctioneer has a microphone so everyone can hear, and some even have video displays to show what item is currently up for bid. Almost all auction houses have a computerized system for keeping winning bids tallied to the right bidder. Some auction houses have a direct link to eBay or other online auctions sites so they can sell their goods "live" to online bidders as well as to in-house bidders.

Then of course, there is the skyrocketing, online auction, eBay, which has changed the face of modern auctioneering and revolutionized the way people buy and sell their assets. People can buy and sell goods across the county and across the globe with a click of the mouse. Now you do not have to wait for an auction, because any time, night or day, you have the ability to search and buy on your computer.

Buying and Selling at Auction

There are a wide variety of auction houses in just about every community in the United States. The eastern part of the county has more auctions than the western part, but some sort of auction can be found just about anywhere. The website Auction Zip, located at http://www.auctionzip.com/, will help you locate all types of auctions in your area.

In the following sections, we will discuss how to buy and sell at the various auction houses. You should locate and visit the auction houses in your area to see how they operate and determine what type of goods sell well and what types do not sell. Remember, at some auction houses you will be competing with other resellers and dealers, but you may also be competing with collectors. It is almost impossible to beat out a collector at an auction. A collector is someone who is buying items for his or her own personal collection and not for resale. The collector is not looking to make a profit on the piece, so he or she will almost always bid higher than a reseller is able to bid.

Also, be sure to check out the terms of each auction house. Most auction houses now charge a buyer's premium, and all charge a commission to sell goods. These charges can vary greatly from one auction house to another.

High-End Auction Houses

I am sure everyone has heard of the exclusive auction houses such as Sotheby's, Bonham's, and Butterfield and Christies. While these are fabulous places, and every auction lover should attend an auction held at one of them, the average reseller will have few opportunities to interact with these historical auction houses. If you are lucky, you will at some point come across a valuable item that is worthy of being auctioned off at one of the famous houses. These auction houses are very discriminating and will only take very fine items to auction.

Buying for resale at such auction houses would be very difficult unless you are buying for a specific clientele with very deep pockets. This method of buying to resell is best left to the experts. Buying to resell at such an auction house would also require in-depth knowledge of the product you are purchasing. This is not the place to learn your trade or the place to go with your gut feeling on an item.

However, when you come across an item that meets the standards of these auction houses' they are great places to get the maximum price for your item. Be sure to research all the fees associated with the sale of your goods. All the major auction houses have websites where you can learn more about their services.

Specialty Auctions

Specialty auctions are those auctions that are held to sell a particular line of goods such as sports memorabilia, art, jewelry, or really just about anything you can lump into a category. Some auction houses hold several "specialty auctions" each year and others just have them when the opportunity presents itself. These auctions can be great places to learn about a particular field and great places to sell your goods that fall into the specialty category.

Most of the specialty auctions attract huge numbers of collectors, so as a general rule, it would not be a place you would want to buy for resale.

Local Auctions

Local auction houses can vary greatly, from the antiques and collectibles auctions to the farm auction and everything in between. The local auction can be a great place to buy and sell your goods. Most areas in the United States will have a wide variety of auction houses from which to choose. Remember, when you buy at a local auction, you are only competing with the local population, but when you sell online, you are selling to the world. When buying, look for items that are not locally popular or in abundance in your area. For example, here in North Carolina there are not many collectors of modern art, but it is hugely popular in other areas of the United States. When modern art is mixed in with other antiques at the local auctions, I can usually get the pieces for a very good price. I buy those items to resell online.

There are certain items you will want to sell at a local auction. Look for items that are hot in your local city or region. Another great thing to sell locally is items that tend not to do very well in online auctions. Furniture has limited success on eBay due to the high cost of shipping. Also, fine jewelry has not taken off on eBay like most other goods. Jewelry sales have improved over the last few years, but many people are still very leery of purchasing fine jewelry online due to all the incorrect or fraudulent information in jewelry listings. Also, look for those specialty auctions to sell locally collected items.

Online Auctions

As I have mentioned before, buying online to resell online is a risky venture unless you are very knowledgeable about what you are buying. Several years ago, Daren and I would search eBay for great deals on certain types of antiques. Sellers are getting better about listing their items correctly, and there are more buyers than ever before shopping online. Since eBay has grown by leap and bounds in recent years, it is even harder to find a great deal, but it can be done. It takes time, and you need to have a narrow field of search. It can take hours to search through even the smallest of categories on eBay, so limit your searching field as much as possible.

I would search for sterling silver deals by looking for people who had misspelled the word *sterling*. There is also a famous maker of silver jewelry and other items whose name is spelled in an unusual way. This Danish designer spells his name Georg Jensen. I often look for items by him that sellers have incorrectly listed under the spellings "George" or "Jenson."

One other tip is to look for new listing with a low Buy- it-Now price. I have never understood why someone would list an antique or collectible as a Buy-it-Now item, but people do. We once found an auction for five sterling bowls at a Buy-it-Now price of $100. Needless to say, we grabbed it and resold every bowl for well over $100 each.

There are other items listed incorrectly, without key or important words in the titles. You need to have a deep knowledge of a particular type of item to be able to pick up great bargains at an online auction. As I said before, it can be a time-consuming pursuit, because you will have to sift through mountains of listings to find the one, true bargain. I have found that, for the most part, there are better places to get good deals, but that does not keep me from looking on occasion.

Selling online is our favorite method for selling items. If you list items correctly, take good pictures, and do all the other things a good seller should do, then the online auction site is one of the best overall places to sell. No other selling format can give you access to millions of potential buyers. But you have to be able to reach those buyers by listing items with the correct key words in the title. Always keep in mind that your title is the only avenue for potential bidders to find your goods. There is no store to browse or clerk to ask, so make sure every word in your title counts, and try to use every space available; eBay allows fifty-five characters in the title. Be sure to use each one, and put in as many key or search words as possible. The title does not have to make sense or be grammatically correct; it has to bring buyers to your auction.

Even with millions shopping on eBay every day, there is a ceiling as to what buyers will spend at the online auctions sites. That ceiling will vary from customer to customer and depend on what types of goods are being sold. The limit to selling online is that potential buyers cannot examine the product firsthand. If buyers cannot see an item and hold it in their hands to confirm the condition and age, they may be less willing to risk large amounts of cash. This ceiling comes into play especially on antiques, collectibles, and jewelry.

Online auctions are great for the vast majority of goods that you will be selling. Goods that are extremely valuable may sell better at a different venue. I cannot give you a certain dollar figure that would be my absolute cutoff point, but as a general rule anything valued over $5,000 should not be sold online. The exception to this guideline is the buying and selling of automobiles. That market is a huge and thriving business on eBay, and it does not have the same constraints as other categories.

Buying online can be more risky than buying at the local auction gallery. When buying online, you are dealing with a stranger, paying online, and depending on the seller to ship you the product. At a local auction gallery, you are dealing with someone who has a brick and mortar place of business. If there is ever a problem or issue with a purchased good, you can easily contact the auctioneer and resolve any issue. While the vast majority of sellers and buyers on eBay are honest people, there are those who are not. In order for the online marketplace to work, there has to be trust between the buyer and the seller. The buyer has to trust the seller to list the item accurately and to ship the item. The seller has to trust that the buyer has not paid with a fraudulent money order or check. By using the PayPal service, the seller has more protection, but the seller also risks the buyer filing a complaint or reversing credit card charges through PayPal.

If you are a buyer on eBay, I highly recommend that you use PayPal to pay for your goods. There is no charge to the buyer to use the service, and PayPal offers a buyer protection service. PayPal will return your money if the seller cannot prove that the item shipped or if the item you received is significantly different than what was described in the listing. PayPal will not cover you for minor problems or issues.

Modern Art Sold in Broad Market

One of my regular customers, who had a small space in an antique consignment store, brought me two small statues to sell. She stated that she had a $50 price tag on each, but she had been unable to sell them. She said they had been sitting in her space for months and she just wanted to get rid of them. With just a little online research, I found that the pieces were made by the 1960s famous British artist, Richard Parkinson. Both pieces were small, black-and-white, modern art sculptures. One was a bust of a girl, and we sold her on eBay for $1001.99 and the other was a bird, which sold for $760.

The pieces did not sell in the consignment store, because the right person did not come in the store looking for modern art sculptures. The antique consignment store specialized in the traditional things you will find in an antique store; thus, few if any modern art collectors ever went into the store. People who are unfamiliar with modern art would not recognize the name Richard Parkinson, so they would pass by the sculptures.

On the other hand, when I listed the pieces online, I was selling to the entire world and a huge modern art collecting audience. In fact, one piece went back to Great Britain, and the other piece went to Colorado. The point is that you want to buy in a narrow field and sell in a broad field.

Storage Facilities Auctions: the Grab Bag of Auctions

It seems like everywhere you look these days, you will see another storage unit facility popping up. It is a testament to American's obsession with hording objects they have no need or space for in their lives. When the storage unit renters do not pay the storage bill, the owners of the storage facility will auction off the contents of the unit to pay back storage fees. You will see all kinds of items inside these abandoned units. The typical unit will usually hold pieces of furniture, clothing, old tools, or stereo equipment. Sometimes there is a gem or two worth bidding on at the auction or buying directly from the storage facility owner.

Many times these storage units were rented after the death of a family member or the renter of the unit died and the heir of the estate failed to pay the monthly rent. These "estate" units can be filled with a virtual treasure trove of great items.

Some of these businesses will have a notification system or mailing list to which you can add your name. Most of the owners go through local auction houses to sell the items, and you can get on the auctioneer's mailing list. Storage unit auctions usually do not attract a lot of people. I have seen as few as four people and as many as twenty people attend these types of auctions. So it is very unlikely you will have a lot of competition.

Every auctioneer is a little different, but the fundamental procedure is the same. The auctioneer and buyers will walk out to the units up for auction, and the lock will be cut and the doors opened. The buyers will take turn walking up to the unit and looking at the contents. Most auctioneers will not allow you to enter the unit or spend a great deal of time pawing through the items. This is why I call them "grab bag" auctions. Sometimes you can get amazing items, but other times the unit will be filled with junk, and it can be hard to tell the difference.

Most of the time, there will be furniture inside the units. If you are not set up to handle furniture, you may want to stay away from buying the entire units. I do not like dealing with furniture unless it is something very special, so I talk to the other buyers at the sale to find out if any of them would like to buy any furniture left in the units I purchase. Most of the people you will find at these sales would love to have the furniture. So if I buy a unit with furniture, I offer it to the other buyers at the auction for an extremely low price, provided they are willing to get it out of the unit that day. It is a great strategy, and if the other buyers know upfront that they can get the furniture from you for cheap, they are less likely to bid against you on the unit. However, do not make deals upfront before the bidding. The auctioneer will not let you work deals with other customers before the bidding begins, but after the auction is over, you are free to sell to whomever you choose.

Before you purchase an entire unit, remember that you will be required to remove all contents of the storage unit, usually within forty-eight hours, and leave it broom-swept clean. So do not buy more than you can handle. You do not want to leave goods in the unit or leave a mess for the facility owner. You will get a reputation as unreliable, and the auctioneer will refuse to sell to you in the future.

Some auctioneers will remove items from the unit and sell them individually or in groups instead of selling the entire unit as one lot. The auction is less risky for the buyer, because you will get a better look at what is up for auction. However, you will still not get a chance to test any electronics or fully inspect any pieces in detail. But that is why the bidding is usually very low.

For this type of auction, you need to have a good overall knowledge and be conservative with your bidding. There are numerous reasons why a storage unit would be abandoned and the contents sold at auction, but the main reason is because the renter does not have the money to pay the storage fees. If the renter does not have the money to pay the storage fees, the things inside may not be worth a great deal of money. That is not to say they are worthless, and sometimes there are things of great value inside, but you need to be careful when purchasing at these grab bag auctions.

The only hint I can give you is to look closely at the items that you can see when the door is opened. If the furniture or items you can see appear to be of nice quality or antique, you may have a winner. If the furniture is of the cheap plywood variety, you may not be looking at the best unit. If the items you see are destroyed, dirty, and generally not in good condition, it is likely the rest of the items will be in poor condition. Also look at the condition of the unit itself. Are the boxes and furniture placed in the unit in a neat and organized fashion or is everything thrown into the unit haphazardly? If everything is thrown into the unit, these people did not care about the items, and the unit's contents most likely are not in good condition or are of poor quality. These are just general guidelines, and there are exceptions to every circumstance, so you will have to let your eyes and experience guide you.

Sometimes the owners of the units will sell outright to people without the benefit of an auction or public sale. This of course can be a goldmine opportunity for an enterprising person. However, keep in mind that the owner will expect you to take everything out of the unit so he can rent the space. I would also highly advise you to look at every unit before you purchase it. I have seen units that only have personal paperwork and old clothing inside, but I have also seen units with silver coins, antique furniture, high-end stereo equipment, and more.

Government and Police Auctions

Another great place to get good deals is at police or government auctions. These auctions almost always require cash and are attended by very few people, and thus, the potential for great bargains is very high. You will have time to inspect and look at all the merchandise, but usually no warranty is given on the items.

The police auctions are usually held two or three times a year to sell off unclaimed recovered stolen property or property that was seized by the police. At these auctions, there will be diamond rings, electronics, cars, boats, and just about anything you can imagine. The auctioneer will sell everything individually or in very small groups.

The government auctions are usually held when the local government wants to sell off its old assets. There will be old computers, office equipment, cars, and building equipment. Depending on what you want to sell, there can be potential in some of these items.

WHOLESALERS

There is no way to sell to a wholesaler unless you are a manufacturer, so in this section we will cover some examples of how to buy from a wholesaler. There is a wide range of wholesalers in most areas. There are manufacturers that will sell at a discount to retailers or individuals. There are liquidators who sell overstocked or out-of-season goods. There are importers who sell goods in bulk. Almost all of these types of wholesalers can also be found online.

There are trade shows for retail buying, at which wholesalers generally sell to retail stores, but they will sell to individuals too. However, as an individual you must still buy a certain quantity of goods in order to get the wholesale price.

You can find out information on these trade shows by going online, or they can be found in retail trade publications. If you decide to pursue this area, be prepared for stiff competition and to spend a great deal of money upfront. We recommend that before you purchase any goods in bulk, you do your research. You should know exactly where you are going to sell your goods and what price the market will bear. Technology-related items can decrease in value rapidly.

I would like to emphasize that, when you are deciding to make a purchase, you should beware of the salesperson. In many buying situations, the salesperson is highly skilled at getting your money and will make you promises to make that happen. He or she is keen to your needs and knows what to say in order to close a deal.

You should also be cautious if you decide to purchase in an overseas market. The pricing is attractive, but it can be a very risky purchase. If you deal with overseas sellers, they will generally demand upfront money. This could be a problematic situation—if something happens to your shipment along the way, you will likely have no recourse. If your shipping terms are Free on Board (FOB), freight collect—which is more often not the case with overseas shipments—the buyer assumes all responsibility

CONSIGNMENT STORES

Consignment stores are gaining popularity across the country due, in part, to the ever-increasing price of durable goods. As the price of goods continues to rise, more and more people are open to the idea of purchasing secondhand items and, even more, people want to receive some return for their slightly-used items. In our local area, over six consignment stores have opened in just the last year. As with many businesses, there is a wide variety of and there are many levels of consignment stores. Most people think of clothing consignment stores, but there are furniture, accessory, and antique consignment stores, as well as a plethora of specialty consignment stores.

The negative to selling through a consignment store is that most take between 40 to 60 percent of the sales price. Also a consigned item can remain in the store for months without being sold. If your item is seasonal or its value is based in technology, this can hurt your profits. And finally, the non-auction format makes it tricky to set a price. If you set the price too high, the item will not sell; set it too low, and you loose money.

I have a few consignment stores to which I take select goods for sale. But instead of putting my goods on consignment in the store, I usually try to sell the items outright to the owner of the store. I only sell very select goods to consignment stores, and I know before I purchase the item that I will be selling it at a consignment store. I also have built a relationship with the owners of the stores, so I know what they are willing to pay. Selling outright rather than on consignment is a personal decision for me; I just prefer to receive the return on my investment right away even if that means I have to take a little less profit. I do not like waiting around for a buyer, and I have so much going on that I would loose track of items sitting at a consignment store for months.

Furniture is the one area where I would recommend using a consignment store. Unless you are or your trading assistant is set up to sell furniture online, then the process is costly and time consuming. To ship anything but the smallest of end tables will require shipping by freight carrier. This requires unusual packing material and relationships with several freight carriers to get the best service and price. Shipping furniture adds a huge cost to the online buyer, so most people avoid buying furniture online unless it is from a major company or seller who specializes in that area and can offer discounts on the shipping due to volume.

As to buying, consignment stores can be great places to look for bargains. As with auction houses, consignment stores can vary as to the type and quality of merchandise they have, so shop around. Some consignment stores will reduce the price of an item after it has been on the shelf for a certain period of time. Also, consignment store operators will usually barter a little bit on the price, especially if you are buying several pieces. Remember this tip from the negotiation section: if you are buying several items from one dealer or store, be sure to ask for the volume discount. The operators or owners of the business may say that the items are on consignment so they cannot offer a discount, but remember the seller can take the discount from his or her end of the price. The consignment store owner usually retains 50 percent of the sales price of an item. Giving you a 10 percent discount when you are buying eight items should not be a problem if the owner wants to make the sale.

Many clothing consignment stores deal in designer label merchandise and will accept only the current fashions. These stores usually examine the goods very carefully, but you should take the time to go over each piece you purchase looking for any flaws. Most consignment stores have a very strict or a no return policy.

Other consignment stores will try and sell out-of-date clothing and goods that have not made it to "vintage" status. Be aware of your market, and avoid any goods whose trend has passed no matter how tempting the price.

TWICE-A-YEAR CHILDREN'S CONSIGNMENT SALES

There is a new, twice-a-year consignment sale that is gaining popularity across the nation. This type of sale, which is usually held by mothers' groups, churches, or some very enterprising moms, is a great place to find high-quality used children's clothing. These groups usually have two sales a year—one for spring and summer clothing and the other for fall and winter clothing. Ask around to find out if there are such events in your community.

The twice-a-year consignment sales works like this: The mothers bring in clothing that their children have outgrown and buy new clothing for the kids at the same time. There are great bargains to be found at these events, and you do not have to sell clothes in order to shop. I have found great deals for my daughter and for resale. The smaller-size clothes are usually plentiful and in the best condition. I know of several women who shop at yard sales for children's clothing all year long and then sell the clothing at the twice-a-year consignment sales. Some of these women make several thousand dollars at each sale! Keep in mind that if you are shopping at yard sales for children's clothing, you can buy any size, but always buy brand-name clothing in excellent condition.

ANTIQUE SHOPS AND MALLS

Antique shops and malls are fun places to go and learn about a wide range of goods, but they are not great places to buy or sell. While it is possible to stumble upon a bargain, we have found it to be a rare event. Most antique shops are owned by people with considerable knowledge of the goods they are selling, and owners price their merchandise at the highest possible value. Unlike online sellers, these dealers have huge overhead costs including the retail space, employees, and utilities. While some of the dealers have begun to sell online, many have not, and they are not realistic about current market values. See our section in chapter four, "The eBay Effect," for more information.

I am sad to report that many of the antique shops and malls are going out of business in our local area. We have had at least three in the greater Raleigh area close within the last two years. Their prices are just too high, their items are too limited, and their locations are not convenient when compared to online shopping.

If any of these places are going to survive, they must price their goods more inline with the online auctions. After all, if I am in a store, and I know an item is priced equally or close to what I can buy it for online, then I will certainly buy it at the local store. By buying at a local shop, I would not have to pay the shipping fees associated with online buying, and I would be able to examine the piece for myself.

As with any type of store, antique shops can vary greatly, and you should visit the stores in your local area to determine if they are viable options for purchasing goods. Almost all antique stores and shops will barter on the price. But owners will usually only bargain within a 10- to 20-percent range, which is usually not enough of a bargain to enable you to buy items for resale. However, at antique stores, you may find goods you would like to purchase to add to your own collection, and you will most certainly increase your knowledgebase.

ESTATE SALES AND TAG SALES

The terms *estate sale* or *tag sale* are usually reserved for sales at which you can find items that are considered to be antique or collectible. An estate sale usually refers to the sale of the majority of goods that were owned by a person who has recently died. A tag sale can be held by someone who is just downsizing or relocating, but it also usually refers to the sale of the vast majority of a person's (or family's) goods. These sales are usually held by specialists or professionals, although family members can hold the sales themselves. The specialists are responsible for pricing and holding the sale as well as disposing of any unsold goods after the sale. Usually the sale is held for two to four days with the price of goods decreasing over the days. Estate and tag sales can be an important source of goods for the dealer or reseller.

If you have goods you want to sell at an estate or tag sale, you either have to have a lot of items or be willing to include your items with another person's tag sale. Sometimes the person who is running the sale will take extra goods to sell at an estate sale.

Choosing a reputable and knowledgeable specialist is the most important consideration when deciding to sell your goods at a tag sale. Make sure the person who you hire understands the items you are selling and the amount of money you need to gain from the sale. Plan to discuss each item of significant value, and make sure that he or she understands the importance or history of the piece. *No person can know everything about all antiques and collectibles, but a specialist should have a broad knowledge of antiques in general.* A specialist should be willing to talk with you about the items and discuss the pricing of the goods. If you plan to give the estate or tag sale specialist repeat business, he or she may be willing to give you a discount on the commission especially if your items are lumped in with another sale. It never hurts to try to negotiate the seller's commission. I will, on occasion, reduce my selling commission for repeat customers if they have high-quality goods.

Buying Tips for Estate Sales

Estate and tag sales can be a great place to purchase goods for resale. In one location, you have access to a wide range of goods, which should be better quality than those you find at flea markets and yard sales. Most tag sale specialists price their goods for reasonable amounts, but sometimes you can get an extremely good deal. I try to go to the sale the very first moment that it opens and scoop up any great deals. Then I return on the last day to get huge discount prices on the items that were priced too high to sell on the opening day. Here is a great tip. *Instead of waiting for the last day of the sale to negotiate bargain basement prices, go at the end of the day on the next to the last day of the sale.* This will put you ahead of any person arriving the last day of the sale looking for discounted items.

For example, if the tag sale is being held on Friday, Saturday, and Sunday, you would want to go early Friday morning to purchase any goods that are marked at bargain prices. Sunday is the day the tag sale specialist will mark down the items. Instead of waiting until Sunday when all the other bargain hunters return, return on Saturday thirty minutes before the end of the sale day. Specialists know that they will be slashing prices as soon as they close for the day, so they are very willing to negotiate at this point. Also, keep in mind that, if you have more than one item to purchase, the seller will be more willing to reduce the price.

Tag sales can be held in different ways. Sometimes the merchandise is left on the table and half of a tag is removed to show that it has been purchased. You take your pulled tags to the checkout area, and someone will retrieve and pack your purchased goods. Most times, though, you just enter the sale and grab hold of anything you wish to purchase. It may be a good idea to carry a laundry basket or other container so you can hold all the items you wish to purchase. Be sure to check with the person running the sale to make sure it is OK to bring in such items. Sometimes the rooms are so crowded that it may not be possible to carry around a large basket.

There are usually just a handful of professionals who hold estate and tag sales in a particular area. It is a good idea to get to know these people and get on their mailing lists. Attend their sales, and research their pricing. You will learn which specialists price their items too high and which price too low. You will learn which specialist will deal on goods and which will not. If there is more than one person pricing, you will also learn who is softer on negotiation, so you can always direct you pricing questions to him or her. If you become a steady customer, sellers may let you into the tag sale early, offer you larger discounts, and direct you to great bargains. Remember that the specialist has to earn a living too, and do not expect to get the items for garage sale prices.

We have found that at most tag sales there is a huge variation in pricing. At the same sale, we have found items priced at a fraction of their value and items priced at double or triple their value. As we have said before, the operators of the sale cannot possibly know everything about all antiques, and they will not have the time to research every little thing that is up for sale. So they sometimes just guess at what the price should be for an item. Sometimes they guess too high, and the overpriced item will be discounted in the final day, and sometimes they guess too low, and the item will be a great bargain for whoever arrives first.

As with any purchasing situation, be cautious and have a good idea of the resale value of an item before you purchase it. On the morning of the first day, do not expect to get a discount on your purchases unless you are purchasing many items or very expensive items. However, toward the end of the sale, if the operator of the sale does not offer substantial discounts then walk away.

Sales Run by the Family

Some of the best estate and tag sales are those that are run by the surviving family. Most of the time, the family is in a hurry to get rid of the items or is unfamiliar with the value of the goods. Daren and I have found exceptional bargains at these types of sales. Most of the time, these estate sales are managed more like a yard sale except the merchandise is of much better quality.

No matter what type of tag sale you attend, be sure to carefully examine all the items before you purchase. There is usually a number of items that are damaged, so do not let the excitement of the sale deter you from close inspection of your goods. Do not expect to be able to return any goods after purchase. Everything purchased at a tag sale is usually sold as is with no returns.

PAWN SHOPS: HOME OF THE PROFESSIONAL BARGAINER

Pawn shops are mankind's oldest financial institution, and they can be traced back to ancient China as well as to the ancient Greek and Roman civilizations. Indeed, pawn-broking has an interesting history, which includes the legend of Queen Isabella of Spain pawning her crown jewels to finance Columbus's voyage to America.

One of the earliest recorded pawn-broking institutions in Europe is the House of Lombard. The House of Lombard is said to have had King Edward III as a client during the fourteenth century. The House of Lombard's family crest, which featured three golden balls, has been the symbol of the pawn-broking business for many centuries.

When European settlers arrived in America, so did the pawnbrokers. At the time, pawnbrokers were the major source of consumer lending in the new world. As the banking industry grew, the pawnbrokers played less of a role in major transactions, but they still provided many consumers with loans that were too small for the banking industry. Pawn-broking also provided a lending venue for people with less-than-stellar credit ratings.

Today, the pawn-broking industry suffers from an image problem. Many people think that pawn shops only deal in overused, broken-down items or that they trade in stolen goods. Nothing could be further from the truth! The pawn industry is heavily regulated by the state. A record of every item that is purchased or pawned must be given to local law enforcement. Pawn shops are also regulated by the Office of Consumer Credit and Law Enforcement on a local and national level. While very few stolen items are pawned, any that slip by are quickly discovered and seized by law enforcement. When stolen goods are seized by the police, the pawnbroker loses the money that he or she paid to the person who pawned the item. So it is in the pawnbroker's best interest to avoid stolen goods. The national average of stolen goods received by pawn brokers is under 4 percent annually.

Also, a pawnbroker is unlikely to take goods that are damaged or in poor condition. After all, pawnbrokers are investing their money in the goods, and while 70 to 80 percent of all pawned goods are redeemed, brokers are not going to take the risk of investing in items they cannot resell. All the items are inspected before the purchase or loan is made to make sure they are in working condition.

There are approximately fifteen thousand pawn shops operating in the United States today, so you are very likely to have a pawn shop within your local area. Pawn shops can be great places to buy some goods, but they are not great places to sell your items. Pawn shops not only make loans using durable goods as collateral, they will also buy items outright from customers. Pawn shops usually deal in very specific areas such as jewelry, gold, silver, tools, musical instruments, and electronic equipment. There are those pawn shops that will take just about anything—take a trip to a Las Vegas pawn shop, and you will find the most interesting items—but most shops stick with the basics.

Trying to resell your goods to a pawnbroker is not the best avenue. Pawnbrokers are very shrewd, expert negotiators, and they know the value of everything they deal in on a regular basis. Now you may get lucky and find an employee who knows very little or catch a broker in an extremely good mood, but I would not count on it. The only exception I would make is for gold or silver items that you want to scrap. This would include broken jewelry and other scrap pieces the only value of which lies in the material from which they were made. There are only a handful of melting plants for precious scrap metals across the United States. If you are only going to have the occasional item to scrap, then it is just easier and more convenient to scrap through a local dealer such as a pawnbroker. You will certainly not get the best price for your gold or silver, but remember that your time is also valuable. There are companies that allow individuals to mail in their scrap gold and silver, but be sure to read the fine print. Many of these companies have minimums and charge service fees.

Pawn shops can be a great place to buy goods for resale. I know of a man who purchases musical instruments at pawn shops and resells them at his retail store and on eBay. He knows a great deal about musical instruments, and, over the years, he has developed very good relationships with the area pawnbrokers. Pawnbrokers take in a lot of musical instruments, making them a never-ending supply for this retailer. Also, on average, a pawnbroker will pay approximately one-quarter of the resale value for an item. (Note that I said *resale* not *retail* value.) So pawnbrokers can sell the instruments for one-half or three-quarters of their resale value to the man with the retail shop and still make a profit, and they get to move their merchandise and recoup their investment in the process. The man with the retail shop can charge the full resale value at his retail shop or on eBay, and he will make money. It is a winning situation for both parties.

Over the years, I have noticed that pawnbrokers are getting more involved with selling online and thus less agreeable to selling merchandise at bargain prices. Several years ago, I could go into pawn shops and purchase sterling silver flatware or hollowware at just above scrap prices. Pawnbrokers purchased the sterling flatware below silver market price in anticipation of scrapping the pieces and turning a small profit. I knew the real value of the flatware was not just in the silver it was made of but in the pattern and the maker of the pieces. I would pay pawnbrokers just above scrap prices, which was more than they would get at market, and then I would resell the pieces on eBay at sometimes ten times what I'd paid. I once purchased several Tiffany serving spoons from a broker at $15 each. I then sold each spoon for over $100 on eBay.

I have noticed recently that many pawnbrokers are registered users on eBay, and they are very quick to tell me they can sell whatever item I'm interested in on eBay for more than I am willing to offer. There are many small or small-town pawnbrokers who have yet to catch the eBay fever and many more still who do not want to be bothered with selling on eBay. As any pawnbroker will tell you, pawnbrokers' main income is from the interest and handling fees they charge their customers, not from the items they sell on eBay. Online sales are a tiny sideline to a pawnbroker's real business and a way to move merchandise out of the store. So visit your local pawn shop and see if there is anything you believe has resale potential. Pawn shops should be willing to deal; in fact, pay no attention to the price on the sticker. Pawn shops will usually have a thirty-day guarantee on their merchandise, but be sure to inspect anything you buy, as you would any item you purchase.

CLASSIFIED ADS AND ONLINE ADS

Typical newspaper classified ads are the dinosaur of the reselling industry. The audience is limited to the local population that subscribes to the newspaper and that portion of it that actually reads the classified ads. That is not a large group to market your goods to, and placing an ad is expensive compared to advertising in other marketplaces. If the only way I had to sell an item was through the classified ads section of my local newspaper, then I would not purchase the item.

As to buying, the classified ad is a source of potential goods, but it is a limited one. It takes very little time to browse the classified section of the newspaper, so it is worth a quick scan. If you find anything of interest, be sure to negotiate the price, because anyone using the classifieds as a way to sell an item is clearly desperate and out of ideas.

Online classified ads are growing in popularity. The most notable one is Craig's List. This is a large marketplace where you can potentially buy goods from all over the country; however, you can search by city for goods. We have found a few good items on Craig's List at reasonable prices. I think the online classified site is a good source for products, and it may become a great source in the future.

I would warn people about scams and frauds in both selling and buying on these sites. Buyers will send fake money orders for over the amount and ask you to return the overpayment to an accomplice. There are also sellers who will receive your money and disappear. I would never send money through the mail for goods purchased through online classified pages such as Craig's List. The website has no protections for buyers and no rating system for sellers like eBay and other online auction sites. I would limit my searches to my local area so I could meet the seller face to face and inspect the item before purchase. The only way I would send money to a seller on Craig's List is if he or she accepted an online payment service such as PayPal or BidPay. These online payment services offer a level of protection for the buyer in the case that a seller does not ship the goods.

As for selling items on Craig's List, I believe that the market is still limited, but it could be beneficial for selling large items such as furniture, large appliances, or any goods that are too large or heavy to reasonably ship. In general, I try to stay away from large items, because they are such a headache to ship, but sometimes a deal is just too good to pass up. If I know a large item is going to put several hundred dollars in my pocket, then I will make the effort.

GARAGE OR YARD SALES

Open up your local newspaper, and you will find thirty to fifty listings for yard sales every weekend during the spring, summer, fall, and, depending on where you live, the winter too. We have found that less than half the people who hold yard sales go to the trouble of advertising the sale in the paper. Most just put up a sign at the end of their street and pile their unwanted goods on the front lawn. If you have never been to a yard sale, you may not understand the draw. You may be wondering why people would get up at dawn to drive all over town just to sift through other people's discarded items. The answer can be summed up in one word—bargains.

The Newspaper Challenge

Both Daren and I frequent garage sales, and the items that we find and the prices we pay are unbelievable. Most people think that amazing bargains can no longer be found at yard sales and find it hard to believe that we get a large part of our secondary income from yard-sale resells. People find it so unbelievable, in fact, that a local newspaper reporter challenged my husband to prove it.

The reporter tagged along with Daren one Saturday morning while he made his yard-sale rounds. The results were typical, and a very nice article appeared in the *Raleigh News and Observer* on May 9, 2004. The reporter recorded the items that Daren had purchased that Saturday morning, on which he'd spent $137. The following week, the reporter watched our eBay auctions and noted that the items Daren had purchased sold for a total of $434.21. Daren had made a profit of $297.21, which is not bad for three hours of work on a Saturday morning. This newspaper story can be found on our website, located at www.ebizAuctions.com.

There still may be doubters out there who have been to yard sales and found nothing but a bunch of useless junk. I will have to confess that a lot of the sales we attend are just that. But most people who go to yard sales are looking for things for their personal use, not for resale. When you go to a garage or yard sale with the intention of buying items for resale, your scope is much broader, and therefore you are more likely to find something of value.

You are not going to find something at every yard sale you attend. In fact, by my own, very unscientific research, I have found that about one in every five yard sales has some decent merchandise. So that means that, if you go to twenty yard sales on a Saturday morning, you will find something worthwhile at about four sales. I have had Saturday mornings where every sale I stopped at had some great items, but I have also had some mornings where I have been out all morning and have only found one or two things. You will get frustrated at some point, but remember to keep your scope broad, your options open and set out with the purpose of finding things for resale and not just for yourself.

Helios System

Daren purchased a Helios oxygen system to resell on eBay. The Helios system is a portable oxygen system that allows people with a respiratory illness to travel. We have no need for such a system, so if Daren had just been going to yard sales to buy things for us, he would not have purchased the item. Since he was going specifically with the intention of buying goods to resell, this item was a prefect thing to purchase. He purchased the system for $20 and resold it on eBay for $310. He knew that medical equipment is very expensive, so he was fairly sure he could turn a profit on the $20. When we looked up the system, we found that, if purchased new, it would cost between $1200 and $2000! So we were able to make a nice profit on a purchase, and the person who bought the system from us on eBay got a great deal on a slightly-used system.

Still not convinced? Look to the graphs included in this book. We have a graph that shows all of our purchases from yard sales, flea markets, and auctions during the two months of August and September 2006. We recorded the price we paid for the items, the price each item sold for on eBay, and all the fees associated with each sale. We included actual purchases of everything we purchased that morning. You will notice that not all of the purchases are home runs. On some of the purchases, we barely broke even or made just a few dollars. We wanted to give you a realistic picture of how the system actually works.

The Texas Challenge

My mother, who lives in Texas, would always say to me that she never finds anything at the yard sales near her, and the yard sales in Raleigh must have better things. Since we are always up for a challenge, we decided to try yard-sale reselling in Texas. During a visit to my parents, we set out to prove my mother wrong.

On a Friday morning, we purchased a lot of vintage toys, an Art Deco clock case, a Snap-on Diagnostics tool, a vintage vase, and a vintage sterling and turquoise bracelet for a total of $33. We sold the vintage toys for $151.33 and the clock case for a disappointing $15.59. The Snap-on tool did very well at $112.45. I kept the vase and the bracelet. They were very nice, and getting great things is one of the side perks of this business. Daren accuses me of cutting into his profits when I pilfer his purchases for myself, but a lot of the time I will enjoy the items for a while then sell them.

Even with my pilfering, we sold the items for $279.37 for a net profit of $246.37. We did have to pay $40 to ship everything back to Raleigh so we could list the items, but even with the extra shipping cost we made over $200.

During that morning out, we did limit ourselves, because we knew we would have to incur the cost of shipping the items back. Had we been local, we would have purchased a lot more.

I hope I have convinced you that garage sales can be a good place to obtain products for resale. Having said all the above, I do want to caution you not to be too optimistic. You will drive up to many yards sales and walk away with nothing. You have to keep in mind that we deal in volume, and if you go to ten to thirty sales on a

Saturday morning you should find something of value to resale. Some weeks, you will come home with a car full of incredible purchases, and some weeks you will come home with almost nothing. Also, give yourself time to train your eye to find items for resale. It is natural for your eye to be drawn to items you find appealing but not necessarily ones that will generate the most profit. Even after years of practice, when Daren and I attend sales together, we will be drawn to different things. When we meet back up after perusing the sale, one or the other of us will almost always remark, "Wow that is a great piece. I cannot believe I did not see it first!"

Over time, you will also begin to know which neighborhoods have the best yard-sale items. If you are more interested in selling high-quality, slightly-used goods, then the upscale neighborhoods may be the best place to start. However, if you are interested in selling vintage or antique items, you may want to head to the older neighborhoods where older folks are downsizing or retiring to smaller homes.

Date Sold	Venue	Ebay Number	Description	Purchase Price	Sale Price	Profit	eBay Fees	Net Profit
			SALES FOR AUGUST 2006					
4-Aug-06	GS	230012835362	Vintage Valmazan Cigar cigarette Silver Coin Ashtray	$ 1.00	$ 9.99	$ 8.99	$ 1.96	$ 7.03
4-Aug-06	GS	230020303341	Kawasaki 6" Portable DVD Player #PVS-166W	$ 10.00	$ 32.25	$ 22.25	$ 3.84	$ 18.41
4-Aug-06	GS	230013148288	Brown Leather English Saddle w/ pad & fittings Jumping?	$ 40.00	$ 52.01	$ 12.01	$ 5.15	$ 6.86
4-Aug-06	AUC	230012856311	Edward Chase Watercolor Assault Triple Crown race horse	$ 24.00	$ 162.50	$ 138.50	$ 11.50	$ 127.00
11-Aug-06	GS	230015313260	74 Pc. 1847 Rogers Bros. Anniversary Stainless Flatware	$ 10.00	$ 76.79	$ 66.79	$ 6.42	$ 60.37
11-Aug-06	ES	230015241116	Harley Davidson Chrome Upper Fork Slider Covers	$ 4.00	$ 9.99	$ 5.99	$ 1.84	$ 4.15
11-Aug-06	GS	230015536654	Venturer CDG/ Karaoke Machine w/ Mics& CD Player	$ 10.00	$ 29.00	$ 19.00	$ 3.56	$ 15.44
12-Aug-06	GS	230015539372	Anitque Vintage Great Dane Oil on Canvas Dog Painting	$ 3.00	$ 36.00	$ 33.00	$ 3.98	$ 29.02
12-Aug-06	GS	230015542501	Spyder Victor semi auto cal 68 Paintball Gun view load	$ 10.00	$ 32.51	$ 22.51	$ 3.77	$ 18.74
12-Aug-06	GS	230015543699	Gucci Modern Art Display Sign Black Grey LARGE Statue	$ 10.00	$ 40.00	$ 30.00	$ 1.51	$ 28.49
12-Aug-06	GS	230015549103	Epiphone Studio 10S Guitar AMP Amplifier 19w	$ 6.00	$ 46.00	$ 40.00	$ 1.67	$ 38.33
12-Aug-06	GS	230015577139	Stainless 4 bottle shot dispensor PARTY Barware -	$ 3.00	$ 11.50	$ 8.50	$ 2.01	$ 6.49
12-Aug-06	ES	230015582790	Murano Modern Art Glass Color silver fleck ruffled bowl	$ 1.00	$ 21.03	$ 20.03	$ 3.12	$ 16.91
12-Aug-06	ES	230015588656	Vintage LANE Triangle Mid Danish Modern Eames end table	$ 15.00	$ 79.00	$ 64.00	$ 6.68	$ 57.32
19-Aug-06	GS	230017991846	94-02 Trans Am Camaro Convertible Top Boot Cover	$ 18.00	$ 177.50	$ 159.50	$ 11.85	$ 147.65
19-Aug-06	GS	230017925330	Eddie Bauer Leather backpack Like New Diaper Bag	$ 3.00	$ 14.50	$ 11.50	$ 2.01	$ 9.49
19-Aug-06	ES	230017926662	Harley Davidson Signal Lights & mixed part lot	$ 6.00	$ 26.00	$ 20.00	$ 3.15	$ 16.85
25-Aug-06	GS	230020119085	1980-96 Toyota Land Cruiser & 89-91 Truck Repair Manual	$ 2.00	$ 10.99	$ 8.99	$ 1.76	$ 7.23
26-Aug-06	GS	230020381466	Yakima SpareRoc Spare Tire bike Rack	$ 20.00	$ 51.00	$ 31.00	$ 5.82	$ 25.18
26-Aug-06	GS	230020383000	Yakima SnowRoc Ski or Snowboard Rack tire mount	$ 15.00	$ 24.99	$ 9.99	$ 3.09	$ 6.90
TOTALS				$ 211.00	$ 943.55	$ 732.55	$ 84.69	$ 647.86

Date Sold	Venue	Ebay Number	Description	Purchase Price	Sale Price	Profit	eBay Fees	Net Profit
			SALES FOR SEPTEMBER 2006					
Sep-02-06	GS	230022726325	1982 MB Electronic Stratego All Pieces MINT complete	$ 0.50	$ 56.00	$ 55.50	$ 5.60	$ 49.90
Sep-02-06	GS	230022730481	2 sets LOT vintage Lego bricks Parts building toys 1960	$ 9.00	$ 13.51	$ 4.51	$ 1.35	$ 3.16
Sep-02-06	GS	230022764560	Pro Line Water Proof Deluxe Insulated Chest Waders	$ 5.00	$ 23.50	$ 18.50	$ 2.35	$ 16.15
Sep-02-06	GS	230022779898	Vintage Skateboard GT Spoiler By Grentec Burbank Calif.	$ 1.00	$ 13.50	$ 12.50	$ 1.35	$ 11.15
Sep-02-06	ES	230022794813	Retro Penguin Hot Cold Server Aluminum Bakelite NEW BOX	$ 0.50	$ 9.99	$ 9.49	$ 1.00	$ 8.49
Sep-07-06	GS	230024918602	Alpine Living Air Purifier Model 880 640 sq. feet coverage	$ 40.00	$ 51.00	$ 11.00	$ 5.10	$ 5.90
Sep-08-06	TS	230024668453	Beretta Shooting Jacket Leather Trim Mens Size XL	$ 26.00	$ 45.00	$ 19.00	$ 4.50	$ 14.50
Sep-08-06	GS	230024875039	Tokina 35mm-200mm f/4-5.6 SZ-X352 camera lens + manual	$ 2.50	$ 10.50	$ 8.00	$ 1.05	$ 6.95
Sep-09-06	GS	230024879072	Camera Lot 35mm Canon AE1 Pentax & Olympus Vivitar lens	$ 15.00	$ 90.65	$ 75.65	$ 9.07	$ 66.59
Sep-09-06	GS	230025273398	Technics Turntable SL-D3 Automatic system record player	$ 10.00	$ 38.00	$ 28.00	$ 3.80	$ 24.20
Sep-16-06	GS	230027373523	2 LENOX China Carolina Pattern Dinner Plates	$ 2.00	$ 28.51	$ 26.51	$ 2.85	$ 23.66
Sep-16-06	GS	230027402557	Tektronix 422 Portable Oscilloscope WORKS - Great Cond.	$ 10.00	$ 24.99	$ 14.99	$ 2.50	$ 12.49
Sep-23-06	AUC	230029726185	Early Goebel Dog Boston Terrier Bulldog decanter Vintge	$ 50.00	$ 93.77	$ 43.77	$ 9.38	$ 34.39
Sep-23-06	GS	230029731596	Acoustic Researc AW811 Outdoor Wireless Speaker	$ 5.00	$ 12.05	$ 7.05	$ 1.21	$ 5.85
Sep-23-06	AUC	230029734291	RCA Victor Model 45-J-2 Phonograph Record Player 45s	$ 25.00	$ 46.00	$ 21.00	$ 4.60	$ 16.40
Sep-23-06	ES	230029740861	Vintage Danny O'Day Ventriloquist Dummy 30" Jim Nelson	$ 10.00	$ 15.50	$ 5.50	$ 1.55	$ 3.95
Sep-23-06	AUC	230029748712	Antique 1920s Black Floral Silk Embroidered Piano Shawl	$ 20.00	$ 130.49	$ 110.49	$ 13.05	$ 97.44
Sep-23-06	GS	230029768283	Sony 2.4 GHz Corded & Cordless Phones handsets	$ 5.00	$ 15.51	$ 10.51	$ 1.55	$ 8.96
Sep-23-06	ES	230031255874	Alvin Sterling Silver Wine water Glass Goblet 6 total	$ 150.00	$ 225.00	$ 75.00	$ 22.50	$ 52.50
Sep-24-06	GS	230030054971	Hitachi Sh-G1000 Color Pocket PC Sprint PDA	$ 20.00	$ 67.00	$ 47.00	$ 6.70	$ 40.30
Sep-24-06	GS	230030073181	Vintage NIKON Camera AF N 6006 w/ 50 mm lens Tamrac bag	$ 16.00	$ 39.01	$ 23.01	$ 3.90	$ 19.11
Sep-24-06	ES	230030099821	Hugh Robert Gnome by Tom Clark Golfer - No Reserve #12	$ 15.00	$ 168.00	$ 153.00	$ 16.80	$ 136.20
Sep-24-06	ES	230030100933	Wizard Gnome by Tom Clark - No Reserve #7 1981	$ 15.00	$ 183.50	$ 168.50	$ 18.35	$ 150.15
Sep-24-06	RET	230032182594	Disney Master Replicas Nautilus 20,000 Leagues Sea NIB	$ 130.00	$ 295.99	$ 165.99	$ 29.60	$ 136.39
Sep-30-06	GS	230032139899	NEW Sharper Image Fog Free Light & Razor Shower Mirror	$ 4.00	$ 15.62	$ 11.62	$ 1.56	$ 10.06
Sep-30-06	GS	230032143712	New Easton Hockey Pants HP X-Treme Sports Gear	$ 5.00	$ 15.48	$ 10.48	$ 1.55	$ 8.93
Sep-30-06	AUC	230032145052	Vintage Frogger & Donkey Kong Table Top Games	$ 14.00	$ 56.09	$ 42.09	$ 5.61	$ 36.48
Sep-30-06	AUC	230032160331	Vintage Western Braided Leather Hide Cowboy Bull Whip	$ 6.00	$ 20.50	$ 14.50	$ 2.05	$ 12.45
Sep-30-06	AUC	230032160332	Huge Atari Lot Base Swtich games joy stick controllers	$ 18.00	$ 23.00	$ 5.00	$ 2.30	$ 2.70
Sep-30-06	ES	230032173120	Vintage Israel Hanukkah Menorah 60s By Hen Holon	$ 5.00	$ 24.50	$ 19.50	$ 2.45	$ 17.05
Sep-30-06	ES	230032178248	Lot Vintage 1968 Annalee Mobilitee Rabbit & Santa Elf	$ 8.00	$ 12.51	$ 4.51	$ 1.25	$ 3.26
Sep-30-06	GS	230032165726	Cox Corsair Engine Powered Control Line Airplane Parts	$ 5.00	$ 44.50	$ 39.50	$ 4.45	$ 35.05
				$ 647.50	$ 1,909.17	$ 1,261.67	$ 190.92	$ 1,070.75

These are the actual purchases that Daren and I made during August and September 2006. We did not add or leave out any purchases that we made. We kept in the great, good, and not-so-good purchases so that you can have a realistic expectation of how your sales may appear.

FLEA MARKETS AND SWAP MEETS

The first recorded mention of a flea market appeared in Paris, France, in the 1860s under the name *marche aux puces,* which translated means "walk to the fleas" or "market of the fleas." The common story is that the outdoor bazaars in Paris were given this name because of the tiny bloodsucking parasites found in upholstered furniture that was put out for sale—which is why, even today, I highly advise against buying used upholstered furniture.

Swap meet is a more recent term used mainly in the western United States, but a swap meet is essentially the same thing as a flea market.

Whatever the term or the history of the flea market, it can be another great source of items for resale—provided you know who to buy from. A lot of people who sell their wares at the local flea markets do not sell online, but that does not mean they do not know the value of their merchandise. The majority of sellers at the flea markets are dealers. It will be almost impossible for you to purchase from a dealer at a price that will make the piece a good candidate for resale. There are always exceptions, but you need to be very careful when purchasing items at a flea market or swap meet. You must know what you are purchasing and have a very good idea of its resale value. Although you have to practice your purchasing skills, be sure to practice on low-cost items so you do not lose too much money if you are wrong about the value of your purchase.

Some of the best salespeople can be found at the local flea markets. Do not let a good sales pitch talk you into a bad purchase. Be especially wary of sellers who say that a particular item sells for two or three hundreds dollars more on eBay. If that were the case, the dealers would be selling the item on eBay themselves. There are many dealers who are honest, but there are just as many who will say anything to make a sale. Use your own eyes and judgment to determine the value of an item. Also, be sure to check for damage before you buy. There seems to be a lot of slightly damaged goods at the flea market. A chip or crack on an item will reduce the value as little as 20 percent or take the value down to zero. It is not the responsibility of the seller to point out damage or defects in the item, so always keep in mind the Latin phrase *caveat emptor,* which means "let the buyer beware."

There are other sellers at the flea market who are not professional dealers and have set up shop for a variety of reasons. These are the sellers you want to seek out. As we have mentioned before, start out buying things you know and slowly expand your areas of knowledge. The flea market can be a very exciting place filled with beautiful and unusual items, but do not get caught up in the moment and make impulse purchases. Use the skills you have learned from previous chapters to think about your purchases and negotiate the best deals for the best products available. Remember this business is about making many good purchases over time and not about buying one item that will make you a millionaire overnight—although that has happened in the past, and I am sure it will happen again.

The best time to buy at the flea market is the opening hours when the booths are still being set up or the last hours before it closes. Being one of the first people in the door gives you a chance to find great pieces before others people have had a chance to snatch them up. A good tactic is to move quickly through the market scanning the booths and tables for items of interest. Early in the morning is not a time to have a lengthy discussion with the booth owners about the merchandise. It is also not the time to haggle over the price for more than a few minutes. Offer a low but fair price; unless the owner comes back with a suitable price, move on and plan to come back later. The morning is the time you need to move quickly and cover as much ground as possible seeking out the best deals of the day.

The other great time to get bargains at the flea market is the last day of the sale near closing time. This may be the only time you can get a bargain from the professional dealers. A lot of sellers would rather sell at a discount than haul unsold merchandise back down to their stores or warehouses. This is especially true if the flea market is only held once a month or if the item is large and heavy to move such as furniture. Always keep in mind that the dealers have to make a living too. They are not going to give away their merchandise, and it is never a good idea to insult the seller with an outrageously low price.

THIRFT STORES

Although there are some for-profit thrift stores, most are nonprofit stores that rely on donated items to fund a charitable cause. The American public is a generous group and is known to donate items of great value to local charities, which is why thrift stores can be a great source of items to resell.

While I always recommend checking out all potential sources of product, you will most likely find that the thrift stores with the best merchandise are the ones closest to wealthy neighborhoods. There are also thrift stores that are connected with hospitals and other prominent organizations and groups so be sure to investigate those stores as well.

While most thrifts stores are loaded with clothing, there are other items of interest too. If selling used designer clothing is an area you would like to pursue, then finding great thrift stores in your area is a must. As with anything, condition is a key factor in determining salability, so be sure to check for wear, stains, and any damage. Also stay away from items that are dated and out of style.

If clothing is not of interest to you, do not worry; thrift stores offer plenty of other merchandise from which to choose. Many stores carry a full range of products including auto parts, tools, household goods, books, furniture, and collectibles. Some thrift stores even have a special section for antique and vintage items. Some of the items we have found at our local thrift stores include Baldwin Brass candlesticks, Waterford Crystal lamps, and sterling silver flatware. Stick to the known, brand-name merchandise and remember that you will have to sort through a lot of junk to find the treasure.

Chapter Twelve
Conclusion

A FEW FINAL THOUGHTS

From Nancy

I hope that most of you are excited and ready to start seeking out bargains to flip, but there may be some of you who are unsure if you can really make money by becoming a Flipster. Let me once again encourage you to try, and reassure you that you can do this. Remember to start out with small investments in items about which you are familiar. When selling online, seek out brand name items, and always look for quality pieces. Avoid items that are damaged or have notice-able wear. Be sure to keep track of all your expenses including shipping costs. Keep track of your successes, because they will encourage you to continue. Keep track of your failures, because they will educate you for future purchases. You will make a bad purchase or two along the way. That is part of the learning process, so do not get discouraged by some small mistakes. However, you should limit your risks, especially when you are a beginner. Nothing will dishearten you faster than losing a large part of your bankroll on a poor purchase.

Many of you may feel that you do not have enough knowledge or experience to attempt to buy items for resale. Do not let that deter you! When I started flipping items on a full-time basis five years ago, I had no more experience or knowledge than any of you. I had worked in large corporations for over fifteen years and hated every minute of it. I had attended auctions and gone to flea markets on occasion, but I had never been in the antiques or collectibles business. When I went to these places, it was merely to seek out something for my personal collection or home.

When I left the corporate world after the birth of my child, I had no interest in returning. However, as my daughter got older, I had more free time and wanted to contribute income to the household. I wanted to work part-time until she reached school age then return to work full time, but I still did not want to return to the corporate world. I was seeking a more fulfilling career, and I stumbled upon it by accident.

We had purchased a few things on eBay, but we had not considered selling on eBay until we decided to clean up our attic. Like the attics of many others, ours was filled with good items that we no longer wanted or needed. Daren knew that having a yard sale would not be the best place to sell our good items, so we decided to give eBay a try.

I took pictures of the items with a white bed sheet as my backdrop and plodded through the first couple of listings. It seemed to take forever to get the first listings completed, but I finally got the hang of it. Since then, eBay has made the process more user-friendly.

I did not have a mail scale at the time so I just guessed the weight of packages, which was a big mistake. After loosing money in shipping several times, I purchased a mail scale.

I was almost surprised at how well my items sold, and I was hooked! Soon, I had cleared out the attic, the shed, and the garage. I then started to sell my daughter's clothing that she had outgrown. As time passed, my family, friends, and neighbors found out that I was selling on eBay and wanted me to sell their items too. They all said they would give me part of the proceeds if I would do everything for them. So I did. Keep in mind, this was in the year 2002 and, at that time, there were no eBay drop-off store franchises and almost no consignment sellers.

My friends and family kept me busy for a while, but I was soon searching for more things to sell. I needed to find a steady source of goods if I wanted to continue to be an eBay seller. That is when Daren suggested that I buy things specifically for resale. He suggested that I go to a few yard sales, estate sales, and auctions looking for items to resell, not to keep. At that time, I was not fond of yard sales. The few I had been to seemed to have nothing but a bunch of old clothes and junk. Of course, I had always gone to sales looking for things that I wanted, but not for resale.

I attended a yard sale at which the owners had some very nice antiques, but the prices that they were asking were too high. So I told the couple that I sold things on eBay and suggested that they give me a call if they wanted to sell any of their items. I wrote my phone number on a piece of paper and gave it to them. It was not very professional, but I thought that I would take a chance. The couple did not call me, but a gentleman who was at the sale followed me out to my car.

He said that he had some antiques and collectibles that he would like for me to sell. I gave him my phone number, and he became my first customer.

This man was a wonderful collector and part-time antiques dealer. He had no formal training, but he had a great eye for quality, which had helped him to create the most fabulous antique collection. He had sold things on eBay himself, but due to his job, he was frequently out of town, and it was difficult for him to keep up with the auctions and shipping. Over the next year, I learned a great deal from selling his items, and it gave me the confidence to start an eBay drop-off store.

Selling for others gave me the chance to expand my knowledgebase without having to invest my own capital in the purchase of goods. Also, the items brought to us, varied greatly, which is exactly what I needed to broaden my education. I also continued, under Daren's direction, to purchase my own items for resale. We've made far more profit from selling our own items that we've purchased then we have from the commission we earn from selling for others.

Soon, I felt that I had enough knowledge to purchase items on my own. Now, when Daren and I go out to the flea market or yard sales, we go alone so that we can cover more ground. In 2005 I became a Certified Property Appraiser so that I could appraise as well as sell items.

As you can see, when I started, I had no special training or gift. What I did have that you do not is my husband and his vast knowledge about purchasing, pricing, antiques, and collectibles. He knows what sells and what does not. He has an amazing ability to be able to predict within 10 percent the sale price of any item at auction. He knows the best places to buy and the best places to sell. What we have done in *Buy It, Sell It, Make Money* is condense all the important things he knows about flipping items into book form so that anyone can become a Flipster. I have put into this book what took me years to learn so that you can start buying and selling items within a few days.

Before I began this journey, I felt trapped in the business world where I received great compensation but no personal satisfaction. I dreaded going to work every day and never felt like I was doing what I was meant to do. Now I love my job and look forward every morning to the new challenges. I am always learning something new, which is one of the most fantastic things about this job. I make great money, but more importantly I feel like I am performing a worthwhile function. I have helped people dispose of estate items when they needed help with all the unwanted assets that they inherited. I have helped elderly people downsize to move to smaller homes and young people raise needed cash. I have also found it very gratifying to find new homes for antique items where they can be appreciated and cared for in a proper manner. I remember selling an antique doll to a woman who was very pleased to receive it. The doll was in a neglected state when it came to us, but I knew the new owner would treat it lovingly. The buyer told me that, when she was a child, she had a doll exactly like the one I'd sold her. She said that it brought back all the wonderful memories she had as a little girl.

I have also found it very exciting to uncover a hidden treasure inside a storage unit or at the bottom of a box at the flea market. Daren and I now compete with each other to see who can bring home the best deals. Being a Flipster is a fun way to make a living, and it also provides you with treasures that you can keep for yourself.

And Daren

When my parents dragged me to the auction every Saturday night, I did not know that I was receiving important education and training that would alter my career and my life. When I was very young, I was not at all interested in the auctions; but as I became older, my curiosity developed, and the treasure hunter in me came to the surface. In those early years, just as an athlete trains, I was in the first stages of training myself to become a buyer. I refer to that time in my life as my "wax on, wax off" years, a reference to the movie, *The Karate Kid*. Just as Daniel was unwittingly learning karate chops as he waxed Mr. Miyagi's vintage cars, I was unknowingly learning to spot quality pieces as I sat in that auction house; for example, I could soon differentiate between a piece of Tiffany glass and a standard piece of glass or a piece of Weller from a piece of McCoy.

When I was a little older, I became a runner for the auctioneer who operated the house my parents visited weekly. A runner is the person who holds up an item for the audience to see and helps the auctioneer sell the item by pointing out any important information such as a maker's name or damage. This is when my education took a giant step forward. I was able to examine the pieces and search for clues that might help the piece sell. An auction has to move quickly, so a runner needs to be able to grab an item and know instantly what is important for the audience to know about this piece. Does the item have a maker's mark? Is the item cut glass or pressed glass? Is it silver-plated or sterling silver? Is there any damage? There is no time for asking questions or hesitation, and missing important features would get you a swift kick in the pants from the auctioneer.

This ability would serve me well in years to come as I made my way through crowded flea markets or yard sales. I can now scan a vendor's booth or a yard sale and, within sixty seconds, determine if there is anything that I may be interested in purchasing.

As time progressed, I realized that I had a knack for buying, so I chose the route of procurement as my professional career. I have worked for several major corporations in various purchasing-related positions and continue to do so today. I also continued my passion for finding treasures by becoming a licensed and certified auctioneer. My many years of purchasing and auctioning have given me the knowledge to understand what will sell, what price it should sell for, and how to negotiate a good price based on market conditions.

Previously we mentioned that a Raleigh newspaper reporter joined me on one of my purchasing trips to area yard sales. This reporter tagged along, because she did not believe that there were true bargains to be found and that we could actually make money off of yard-sale purchases. We proved to her and her readers, without a shadow of a doubt, that you can buy it, sell it, and *make money.*

We now open this invitation up to any city in America: we will come to your town and show you that, in any and every community, it is possible to buy items and resell them at a profit.

In today's market there is such an overwhelming amount of unwanted but valuable stuff that anyone can go to any community and do what we have been doing for years. Let this book be your guide to start you on a new and rewarding journey. It does not matter if you only have a few hours each week to devote to this pursuit. Everybody has a Flipster inside, and you can choose how you want to fit flipping into your lifestyle. I hope that by reading this book you have had your light bulb moment and know that, with a little effort and knowledge, you can live a rewarding and fulfilling life by being a Frugal Luxury Investment Purchaser.

Appendix 1
The Field Guide to Buying

HOW TO USE THE GUIDE

This field guide is intended to provide you with the information and terminology you will need to increase your chances of purchasing items for a profitable resale. The definitions and terminology sections are provided to increase your knowledgebase and as a reference tool.

We have also provided, in almost every category, a "good, better, and best" section that lists brand names and types of items you will encounter in the field. These sections will further aid you in selecting the best items for resale. In them, the category under which a brand name appears is based solely on its potential in the resale market based on a number of variables, including but not limited to the residual value, brand popularity, name recognition, and current market trends as of the printing date of this book. The ratings are *not* based on quality of the goods. In fact, there are several high-quality brands or designer names that are rated lower than their lower-quality competitors.

ART: PAINTINGS, LITHOGRAPHS, PRINTS, AND SCULPTURES

The world of art is vast, and it takes years of study to learn even the basics in this area. There are thousands of artists, both current and historical, whose works people are interested in purchasing, so we will not attempt to list every artist you may encounter. Instead, we will give you a general guideline to direct you toward profitable purchases.

There are a number of websites that can provide information on specific artists. The website Ask Art, located at http://www.askart.com, is a very good source to locate past and present artists. Reading an artist's name on paintings can be difficult, so try variations on spellings to see if you can find a known artist with that name. Then compare the painting you have with the known works and signature of the artist in question. If you have a painting you believe to be of extremely high quality and potentially valuable, you may want to consult with a local art expert.

Every type of art and art object is being reproduced for the mass market, and it will be your job to distinguish between the mass-made items and the true works of art. Sometimes this task will be very easy due to the poor quality and obvious production-line work of the piece. However, there are many very good reproductions on the market, and many pieces are made specifically to trick the buyer into believing that the piece is genuine. As a general guideline, look for signs of age and for details that show that the item is handmade and not produced on a production line. Handmade details would include tool marks, hand painting or a signature. In general look at the overall craftsmanship of the item.

Modern day, mass-produced prints are just about worthless with some very rare exceptions. Today, many of the old paintings, posters, and advertisements are being reproduced by the hundreds of thousands so be very careful when purchasing "old" prints or posters. Be sure the piece you are considering is old and not a modern reproduction.

Also, look at the materials from which the item was made. We will provide you with a good, better, and best rating based upon the materials used to produce the item, how the item was made, and the type of item it is.

Rating Guidelines for Art Products

Good:
Limited-edition prints
Resin sculptures

Better:
Signed and numbered limited-edition print or lithographs
Copper
Bronze-clad items (base metal or plaster covered in bronze)
Alabaster or stone sculptures
Vintage posters

Best:
Original and signed paintings
Bronze
Marble
Silver and sterling silver

Gold Mine:
Any *original* work signed by a known and/or famous artist (original work, not a print or reproduced piece)

Art Terms to Know

aboriginal art. Art made by the aboriginal peoples. Aboriginals are native people of Australia.

abstract art. Art that is not representational of known people, places, or things. The abstraction can vary in degrees from subtle to completely unrecognizable. Abstract art is the opposite of realism. Pablo Picasso is famous for his abstract art.

acrylic paint. A paint that was developed in the 1940s as a substitution for oil paints. Acrylics are more versatile than oils and dry much faster.

alabaster. A white to yellowish stone from the gypsum family. This soft stone is easy to carve and has been used in many sculptures and other art forms. The stone has a translucent quality and sometimes has a light marbling effect.

asymmetrical. A term used to describe a design that is organized so that one side differs from the other or is not in balance with it.

attribute. To associate an art object with a particular artist (done by an art expert). When a work is unsigned or unmarked, an expert may attribute the work to an artist based on other similar works by that artist. When a piece is attributed to an artist, it is not fact but a supposition, to which the degree of accuracy is based on the knowledge of the expert.

avant-garde. Artwork that is ahead of its time or in the forefront of a trend or movement.

bas relief or low relief. A term for a slightly raised decoration or form that extends out of the background of a piece, usually found in ceramics, pottery, sculptures, and silverworks.

Benday. Use of dot patterns to create a print. The process was invented by and named for Benjamin Day, but it was made popular by famous artist Roy Lichtenstein.

bisque. Clay that has been fired without glaze. A bisque piece will have a matte finish and a softer feel than a glazed finish.

block printing/woodblock prints. A printing method in which a carved block of wood or other material is used to create an image. Color is applied to the carved wood and then pressed against a paper surface to create an image. Japanese woodblock prints were very popular in the early- and mid-nineteenth century.

bronze. As an art reference, a sculpture made of the metal, bronze. Some sculptures are made of white metal with a bronze overlay and are much less valuable than their completely bronze counterparts.

canvas. Woven fabric usually stretched onto a frame and used to paint works of art on.

caricature. A comical representation of a person whose features are exaggerated. Caricatures are seen in cartoons, in comics, and at fairs.

celluloid/cel. A drawing—sometimes colorized on a transparent sheet or cellophane medium—that is used to create animation. This process is no longer being used, and some of the vintage and antique cels have become collectibles.

chalk. A medium, with colors or pigments similar to pastels, used to create artwork.

charcoal. A medium of burned wood used to create artwork in shades of grey and black.

chevron. A zigzag or V-shape, which is a popular motif of the Art Deco Style.

contemporary. A term that usually refers to the modern, or current, design style or to the artwork that reflects that style.

crackle/crazing. Tiny irregular lines that form on ceramic or pottery, which is sometimes intentionally created by the artist and is sometimes a result of the aging process. If the piece is crazed by age, it can affect the value of the piece.

edition/limited edition. A marking found on numbered prints, figurines, or other artwork that indicates that a set amount of the artist's work has been or will be produced. The marking usually consists of two numbers, the first being the number of the particular print and the second indicating the total number of the prints produced. For example, the numbers 178/2000 would indicate that a piece was the 178th piece created out of a total of 2000. On rare occasions, the first number is greater than the second number. This usually means there was some error or damage on a certain number of the limited pieces so more were produced to reach the given total. The damaged items are usually destroyed so the limited total remains constant, but the number of the piece (the first number) increases.

emboss/embossment. A raised design on a paper surface created by pressing from the back side out to the front.

engraving. Shallow cuts into metal that create a design, pattern, or wording.

etching. (1) The use of acid to create a design on a glass object. (2) The use of acid to create a design or image on a metal plate, which is then used to produce that image onto paper.

Federal Art Project (FAP), Works Progress Administration (WPA), Public Works of Art Project (PWAP), and Civil Works Administration (CWA). Programs created by the U.S. government during the Great Depression of the 1930s and 40s to create employment for artists (FAP and PWAP) and for workers in the construction and other related industries (WPA and CWA).

figurative/figural. Artwork that represents the true form or likeness of a person, animal, or insect.

folk art. Artistic work usually made by rural and unschooled common people of a nation or region reflecting the traditional culture of that people.

foxing. A yellow to dark brown spotty discoloration that appears on paper. This damage is caused when the artwork or paperwork is exposed to humidity.

fresco. An image or painting that is part of a wall or ceiling and was made in a process by which color is applied to layers of wet plaster. The Palace of Versailles is known for its elaborate frescoes.

giclée. A high-quality printing process that allows for the fine detail of the original painting or image to be captured. This type of work is usually printed on archival paper or fine fabric.

gild/gilding. To apply a thin layer of gold to an object, usually ceramics or fine porcelain and sometimes paintings.

hieroglyphics. An ancient Egyptian system of writing using pictures and symbols.

high relief. A term for a raised decoration or form that extends at least halfway out from the background. High relief is usually found in ceramics, pottery, sculptures, and silverworks.

lithograph/lithography. A method of printing using a chemical process to create an image on a sheet of paper. The process must be repeated for each color used in the final print. The process was first developed in the mid-1800s but has improved over the years and is still a popular method today.

limited edition. See **edition**.

marble. A finely grained metamorphic rock used to create sculptures and other art objects.

marbling. A term that refers to the grains, veins, or streaks in any stone or object made of stone.

marquetry. A technique of inlaying woods in order to form a pictorial image. Marquetry was used in the decoration of furniture in the seventeenth and eighteenth centuries but became a work of art in its own right under the hands of Charles Spindler (1865–1938). Spindler created artwork with wood. Most of the art depicted detailed landscape scenes. His artwork was made for both private homes and public spaces.

medallion. A decorative touch to an art object that is oval or circular with raised designs—many times with a human form in the center.

mural. A large painting or design covering one or many walls usually in public spaces.

oil paint. Paint produced when combining color pigments with linseed oil. The paint is slow-drying, but oil painting is a traditional method, which produces brightness and depth of color.

old master. Usually a term used to refer to the artists of the Renaissance period.

ormolu. (1) A term for gilding a bronze object by applying a thin layer of gold to the piece. (2) The gold powder used in the gilding process.

patina. The sheen or color that develops with age on metal objects such as silver, bronze, and copper. A lovely, deep patina is desired by metalware collectors.

polyester resins/resin. A synthetic liquid that is used as a casting material for sculptures and other art objects. Natural resin is secreted by trees and is usually a translucent, yellowish brown; it can be used in lacquers and varnishes. Amber is a resin that, when in its hardened state, is used in jewelry.

pop art. A 1950s and 60s art movement that received its inspiration from everyday objects and familiar images of daily life. The Campbell Soup can paintings by Andy Warhol are perfect examples of pop art.

poster. Oversized or large printed material usually posted in a public space to announce an event or as an advertisement. Vintage posters are collected as art.

provenance. A record of proof of the history of an art object usually with the record of ownership and place of origin of said piece.

Public Works of Art Project (PWAP). See **Federal Art Project**.

sanguine. A red chalk used for drawing.

santos. Painted wooden figurines of religious icons produced mainly in Latin America.

sculpture. A three-dimensional work of art that can be made of bronze, marble, wood, stone, or resin. The piece can be carved, cast, or molded.

screen printing/serigraph/silk screen. A printmaking process by which the ink is applied to a sheet of silk or other mesh-like material in order to form an image.

soapstone. A soft metamorphic rock used to carve figurines and small sculptures. Soapstone is easy to carve but is also easy to damage due to the softness of the rock.

tapestry. A picture formed by the weaving of thread traditionally done by hand but now being produced by machine. This form of artwork dates back to ancient Greece, Rome, and Egypt.

Works Progress Administration (WPA). See **Federal Art Project**.

CARS VEHICLES, AND PARTS

The largest motor vehicle internet auction site in the world, selling a vehicle every 1.7 seconds, is eBay motors. In 2003, eBay motors sellers sold over 6.7 billion dollars of new and used cars, and that number has continued to increase each year. This and other online sites have given automotive sellers a wider audience than the typical local classified ads. This area of buying and selling is not for the weak at heart. It can involve large cash outlays and high risk if the vehicle has mechanical problems. If you are knowledgeable about cars, this could be a lucrative area.

Websites such as eBay, other online auction sites, and non-auction sites such as Craig's List are all excellent places to purchase vehicles. The sellers on these sites should provide all the needed information such as the year, make, and model of the vehicle for sale. Once you have located a vehicle of interest, you can use an online resource such as Kelley Blue Book or Edmunds, which offer free online values. You can also purchase an annual National Automobile Dealers Association (NADA) guide, which is small enough to place in your pocket.

Selling car, truck, and motorcycle parts is another area that can be very profitable. There are many sellers who sell new and used parts, but the best money can be found in selling vintage parts. As with anything, the better the condition of the item, the better it will sell.

Car parts can be small and simple, such as hood ornaments, or large and complex, such as engine components. Parts that are for widely collected cars, such as Ford Mustangs, will command a higher resale value than parts for a Yugoslavian Yugo. We have found that when car owners sell or wreck their cars, they may still have parts they no longer need. These car owners will part with these pieces cheaply, which means more profit for you when you go to resell online.

A popular market is vintage "muscle" cars, and their parts tend to sell best on eBay, but all cars and car parts will sell. The current popularity, price, and rarity will determine the salability of any car or part.

Motorcycles, scooters, boats, RVs, and just about any other transportation item have pieces and parts that need replaced or repaired, so there is always a market for these items. Buyers are also seeking accessories and upgrades for their vehicles, so do not overlook those items when on your search. Keep in mind the size and weight of the goods you are purchasing. Some of these car parts can be heavy or large, and you do not want to run into shipping or storage problems.

CHINA

China and crystal can be great moneymakers, and these items are readily available at yard sales, tag sales, and flea markets. As with any item, quality sells, but in the case of china, beauty sells better. I have come across some nice sets of good name-brand china that have a pattern that is so ugly it will not sell. Some of the china produced in the 1970s and '80s is not pretty and, thus, not popular today. So look at the back of the plate for the maker's name, but look at the front and note how attractive the piece is as well. There are huge price differences among china, so use our guide to help you make correct and profitable decisions.

China does not have to be old to be valuable. Actually, you can receive more money on eBay for current popular patterns than for the older patterns. As with everything, condition is extremely important. Do not waste your time on chipped and cracked china. There are thousands of china patterns, so it is impossible to memorize the popular patterns. Instead, look for quality makers with pretty, eye-appealing designs.

> Moneymaking tip: Serving pieces are the most valuable pieces in a set of china. So when considering china, be sure to note how many serving pieces come with the set. Remember, serving pieces = money.

Also, keep in mind that there are more people who have china made by U.S. manufacturers than there are people who have china that was made in Europe or other places. So a mid-level U.S. manufacturer's china will most likely sell better than a high-quality European manufacturer's china. Also, people will pay more per piece for smaller lots or groups of china than they will for a full set of china. For example, if you are able to purchase a full set for eight of Lenox china, you may want to break up the set and sell it by the place setting or in smaller groups as opposed to selling the full set in one auction. This is because more people want to add to the china they already have and are not willing to invest in a whole new set. Each place setting may sell for an average of $60 per place setting, and the three serving pieces with the set may sell for over $75 each. If you break up the set, you will have grossed $705 for the set. If you sold the entire set together, it may only receive $500. Be sure to investigate which selling method works best for the particular china you are attempting to sell.

While breaking sets up is generally better, keep in mind that you have to pay eBay fees so you should maximize your auction listings. Unless a piece of china is very expensive, I would sell pieces in small lots rather than one piece at a time.

If you have an unusual set from another country or with no pattern name, you may want to sell it as a full set, because there will not be many people who have that particular china pattern and want to add pieces from it to their collection. Most china produced today will have the maker's name and pattern name on the back of the piece, but if it does not, you will need to find the pattern name in order to make the most profit from your purchase. There are several websites that have huge online reference pages that will help you determine the name of the pattern. The best site I have found is located at http://www.replacements.com/. The site has pattern identification tools for china, silver, and crystal.

The term *Limoges* refers to a geographical location in France where many porcelain manufacturers are located. All of these manufacturers can call themselves "Limoges China," and most have a separate trade name. This area of France has been producing fine china for hundreds of years, and it has a rich and interesting history that is worth reading. I have found that, although most of this china is of a very high quality and is very pretty, it usually does not resell as well as it should. There have been some exceptions, but for the most part I have been disappointed in the online sales prices of Limoges china. Most of the china produced in this area did not have a pattern name printed on the back for identification, and many of the patterns look very similar. The manufacturers have been very prolific over the years and have produced thousands of different patterns. It is hard for the consumer to locate pieces of their china pattern without the name and even harder to make a confident purchase online with just a picture.

Be sure to take a close-up picture of the china pattern when selling online even if you have the pattern name. Make sure your bidders can be confident that the pattern you have is the one they want.

Money-making tip: For china and crystal, the pattern name and the maker's name are very important. When you buy china or glass without that information, ask the seller; if the seller knows, you'll save yourself research time and sell your items for more money with one simple question!

Rating Guideline for China Manufacturers

Good:

Dansk
Eddie Bauer
English Ironstone

Fitz & Floyd
Hall
Heritage
Homer Laughlin
Mikasa
Pfaltzgraff
Steubenville
Syracuse China

Better:

Belleek
Copeland Spode
Dresden
Franciscan
Furnival
Gorham
Iroquois China
Lenox
Limoges
Longchamp
Louisville Stoneware
Metlox
New Wharf Pottery
Nikko
Noritake
Pickard
ROWE
Royal Albert
Royal Crown Derby
Royal Staffordshire
Royale
Spode
Villeroy Boch

Best:

Cliff, Clarice
Hermes
Meissan

Minton
Rosenthal
Royal Copenhagen
Royal Doulton
Royal Worcester
Tiffany & Co.
Wedgwood

CLOTHING AND ACCESSORIES

Buying and reselling clothing is a great way to get started in the online sales business. Clothing at yard sales, thrift stores, and consignment stores is very inexpensive and plentiful, so you can easily find product to sell and invest very little capital. The first and foremost thing to remember about clothing is to buy name brands. Remember, when people are shopping online, they cannot examine the piece for themselves so they feel more secure in purchasing name-brand items. Also, expect to receive only 10–25 percent of the original sales price for a clothing item. So an item that sold for $20 at retail will not be worth your time and trouble to sell online. Buying high-quality, expensive clothing will net you more profits.

Another important factor is condition. Only purchase clothing items that are new or like new. You will find lots of clothing that is new or like new on your search. Many people get clothing as unwanted gifts and never wear the item. There are also many people who are addicted to shopping and let their never-worn purchases pile up in their closets until they have a yard sale. Clothing that is stained or ripped will not sell.

Clothing accessories can sell well online too. Purses, scarves, wallets, and shoes can be great moneymakers. Be careful that you are not taken in by fake brand names, especially on purses. The recently produced fake purses are very convincing and are sometimes hard to spot.

Basic Pointers for Buying Used Clothing

1. Avoid buying worn out, stained, and ripped clothing. There are too many better choices online.

2. Buy only high-quality, name-brand items.

3. Styles, fads, and name-brand popularity change quickly in this category so be sure to keep up to date on *hot* names and trends in the industry.

4. Try selling your clothing in lots. Group together clothing that is the same size and same season.

5. Children's clothing sells the best online.

6. When selling clothing, be sure to give measurements as well as the size. Sizes can vary depending on the manufacturer, and including measurements will make your customer feel more secure when bidding on your items.

7. Always examine and list any problems or defects with the merchandise. If an item is shipped to the buyer with an undisclosed problem, then most likely you will have an unhappy customer and have to pay return shipping. Returns are very costly to the online business entrepreneur.

Rating Guideline for Adult Clothing and Accessories

Good:

Adidas
Calvin Klein
Dana Buchman
Eddie Bauer
Gap
Lacoste
Liz Claiborne
Nautica
Nike
Nine West
Old Navy
Talbots
Timberland
Tommy Bahama
Tommy Hilfiger
Under Armour
Urban Outfitters
Van Cleef & Arpels
Vera Bradley
Victoria Secret

Better:

Abercrombie & Fitch
Anne Klein
Anne Taylor
BCBG Max Azria

Banana Republic
Bebe
Birkenstock
Burberry
Christian Dior
Coach
Cole Haan
Diesel
Donna Karen New York (DKNY)
Dooney & Bourke
J. Crew
Jones of New York
Juicy Couture
Luella
Mephisto
Michael Kors
Misook
Oakley
Ralph Lauren (Purple label is best)
St. John
Vera Bradley

Best:

Armani
Channel
Christian Louboutin
Chloe
Diane von Furstenberg
Gucci
Hermes
Jimmy Choo

Kate Spade
Manolo Blahnik
Prada
Versace
Vuitton
Yves Saint Laurent

COINS AND PAPER MONEY

The bad news is the vast majority of circulated coins you will encounter will be worth very little. The good news is there are a few coins waiting to be found that are worth hundreds or perhaps thousands of dollars. There are coin books that are updated every year, which provide book values for every coin manufactured. When determining the value of a coin, you must consider the condition, age, and rarity of the coin. Where the coin was struck is a huge consideration. The mint mark make can be the difference between a $2 coin and a $2,000 coin.

The most valuable coins are those made of precious metals such as gold and silver. Some coins are more valuable because a mistake was made during the striking of a coin. Coins representing a country that is no longer in existence can also be worth your attention. Study the terminology below to help you find coins and properly list any coins you may purchase. A coin's condition can be graded by a professional grading company.

Collecting paper money is another very diverse field of collecting. There are wonderful and interesting historical examples that collectors are seeking. Confederate money is very popular in the United States and, depending on the piece, can range in value from a few dollars to several thousand dollars. Foreign bills are also prized by certain collectors so be sure to look for and consider purchasing old paper money.

Coin Collecting Terms to Know

bullion. Gold or silver in the form of bars or ingots.

bust. A portrait on a coin, usually the head or bust of the leader of the country from which the coin originated.

circulation/circulated. Coins that are circulated within the population for use.

curating. A cleaning method for coins that does not hurt the coin's surface.

deep cameo. A phrase used to indicate that a coin's design—usually the bust of a leader or sovereign—is more raised than normal and may have a frosted appearance. Having a deep cameo can make a coin more valuable.

dies. Metal pieces used to make the coin or imprint the design on the coin.

device. The coin's design, such as the head of a leader, an eagle, or lady liberty.

gold certificate. Paper currency issued by the U.S. government between 1865 and 1933 that is redeemable for gold in the stated amount.

grades. Designations that rate a coin's condition. Coins are graded as follows:

Perfect: Absolutely flawless

Gem Uncirculated: Amazing original luster and virtually no surface flaws

Uncirculated: Original mint luster with no trace of wear

Extremely Fine (XF or EF): Very light wear on only the highest points

Very Fine (VF): Light to medium wear; all major features are sharp

Fine (F): Moderate to heavy wear but with design clear

Very Good (VG): Well worn; design clear, but flat and lacking details

Good (G): Heavily worn; design and legend visible but faint in spots

About Good (AG): Outlined design; parts of date and legend worn smooth; major wear

Fair (Fair): Extreme wear; only some elements are identifiable

Poor: Massive wear; barely identifiable

ingot. A mass of metal in block form.

legends. The words or phrases on the surface of coins.

mint. Physical places where coins are made. Most coins will indicate where the coin was made by the mint mark.

D: Denver, CO

S: San Francisco, CA

W: West Point, NY

P: Philadelphia, PA

C: Charlotte, NC

CC: Carson City, NV

D: Dahlonega, GA (used only for gold coins minted 1838–1861)

O: New Orleans, LA

obverse. The "heads" side of a coin.

off center. An error in the manufacture of a coin that renders it without part of the design. The design of the coin was struck off center thus the coin is missing part of the design. This error can make the coin more valuable since most coins that were struck incorrectly were never released to the public.

over strike/double strike. An error made during the manufacturing of a coin that gives it a double design. This occurs when a one coin is accidentally struck twice creating a double-vision effect on the coin.

planchet. A blank round piece of metal used to make coins.

proof. Coins that are created for the collector. The coins are highly polished and usually come in a sealed case.

reverse. The "tails" side of a coin.

silver certificate. Paper currency issued by the U.S. government between 1878 and 1963 that is redeemable for silver in the stated amount.

troy ounce. A unit of measurement for precious metal, which is heavier than the ounce to which we are accustomed. The troy ounce is approximately 1.1 regular ounces.

uncirculated. A coin that has not been circulated to the population or used as currency.

COLLECTIBLES, DECORATIVE

While there are a few hand-painted and handcrafted collectibles on the market today, the vast majority of them are not handmade. The modern day collectible's price is based upon the marketing machine behind it. That is to say, there is no intrinsic value in the objects—no gold or silver or even fine porcelain. They are not handmade or handcrafted but mass produced by the thousands or sometimes millions. What drives the price of these objects is the population's desire for them, and when that fades, so does the resale price of the goods.

There are some long-term players in the collectibles game such as Goebel and Disney whose products have been and are still desired by a great following, but they are the exception. Of course, even the modern day Goebel Hummel and Disney figurine value drops considerably once you leave the store. Any modern-made collectible's value will be much less than the retail price and will not rise again for many years if ever. Most people who purchase collectibles are not purchasing them to make a profit in the near future but because they enjoy them.

Do not be fooled by the "limited-edition" marketing that is attached to many of these items. The limit is usually very high, sometimes fifty thousand or more. Also, the companies make so many different pieces that there is more product on the marketplace than there are consumers to purchase it. The Disney Company is a master at this marketing. Disney makes a Mickey Mouse figurine holding a ball, and it is a limited edition of fifty thousand. The next year, the company makes a Mickey Mouse walking a dog, and then the next year it releases a Mickey singing a song. Disney does the same thing with every character every year. How many Mickey Mouse figurines is the average person going to purchase? Of course, there are some people who will have thousands of these figurines, but most people do not have the money or space to buy several Disney figurines every year. There is just too much product on the secondary market to keep prices at or above retail.

Collectibles have a huge resale market, but you have to make certain you do not pay too much for the items. Be sure you know your market and resell the items before the market changes. Stick to well-known brands, and try to purchase early editions, first runs, and retired pieces. There can be a huge difference in prices within a series. For example, the very first Hallmark Frosty Friends ornament sells for between $500 and $600. The other ornaments in the series of the Frosty Friend ornament sell for around $30.

Rating Guideline for Decorative Collectibles

Good:

All God's Children
Blue Sky Clayworks
Bradford Exchange
Byers
Charming tails
David Winter
Dept. 56
Disney (some better and best)
Dreamsicles
Duncan Royale
Enesco
Fitz & Floyd
Homco
Lefton
Tom Clark (some better)
Wade

Better:

Anri
Christopher Radko
Danbury Mint
Disney (some good and best)
Hallmark (some best and good)
Goebel (some best)
Lilliput Lane
Melody in motion
Precious Moments (some good and best)
Royal Copenhagen
Reuge
Schmid
Sebastian
Tom Clark (some good)
Willitts

Best:

Armani
Boehm
Cybis
Disney (some good and better)
Faberge
Goebel (some better)
Halcyon Days
Hallmark (some better and good)
Harmony Kingdom
Herend
Jay Strongwater
Longaberger
Precious Moments (some good and some better)
Royal Doulton
Swarovski

CRYSTAL, ART GLASS, AND GLASSWARE

Yard Sale Wedding Gifts

As I got out of my car and walked along the sidewalk, my eye caught the sight of the familiar Waterford Crystal, dark greenish blue box. I made a beeline over to the table, opened the boxes, and found four perfect—never used—goblets, two in each box. The boxes were marked $10 each. I walked over to the young lady running the sale and struck up a conversation.

"These look like they have never been used," I said.

"They were a wedding gift, and we never even took them out of the box," she replied.

"Do you have any other wedding gifts that you would like to sell?" I asked hopefully.

She pointed out a few other items on the table that did not hold much interest for me, but then she said she had some china in the house that she may sell. She had only received a few place settings for wedding gifts and could not afford to buy the rest of the service to complete the set. The sets were Lenox and had a lovely pattern. She sold me three complete place settings for $40, and she had two more Waterford wine goblets inside the house, but they did not have the box so I got them for $5.

What a bargain. I sold the Waterford goblets for approximately $90 dollars a set, $60 for the ones without the box. The Lenox china turned out to be a very popular pattern, and I receive over $120 for each set. I paid the woman a total of $65; then I turned around the next week and sold the items on eBay for over $600. This is why I drag myself out of bed at 6:00 AM every Saturday morning.

There are a lot of unmarked glass and crystal pieces in the marketplace. However, if a piece is marked, the mark will almost always be etched in the glass. The mark can be very difficult to see, but most of the time it is on the underside of the piece. Sometimes the mark is on the side or in another hard-to-see place such as down in one of the design cuts. Because marks are so hard to see, you must hold the piece up at an angle to the available light. A mark usually is a sign of quality.

Many crystal pieces have paper tags, and once the tags are removed, the maker's name can be lost forever. If you are planning on selling your purchases at an online auction site, then it is important to know the maker of a piece. Buyers have to search by name in order to find your items, and they want to feel secure in their purchase. Remember, there is no browsing online like there is in a retail store. A buyer cannot see or hold the piece. They rely on description and pictures. If you have a piece of signed Lalique crystal, the buyer knows exactly what he or she is purchasing. However, if you have a very nice piece of unmarked crystal, most buyers will not even find your piece in order to bid on it much less feel secure in the quality to make a substantial bid. So it is best to buy brand-name items to sell online and sell other quality glass at local auctions or other places.

There are several types of glassware that you will find during your search. The majority of glass you will find will be inexpensive pressed glass. Pressed glass is made from a mold and is usually not very valuable. Pressed glass is smooth to the touch, the pattern is dull not crisp, and the piece is usually heavy. Some vintage pressed-glass pieces can have value, such as those made by Heisey, but most are difficult to sell. See our guide below for examples.

Cut glass is glass that has a pattern cut into the piece. When you run your fingers over the pattern it will feel sharp and crisp. This is a more expensively made item, but without a maker's name, this glass can also be a hard sell online. However, quality cut glass will sell nicely at local auctions or other venues.

Blown glass pieces are made of glass that has been handcrafted and blown into its final shape. This glass usually has tiny air bubbles and is light. Blown glass usually means the piece is of high quality.

Crystal is a type of high-quality glass that contains varying amounts of lead. Crystal pieces can be pressed, cut, or blown.

Moneymaking tip: Be sure to charge the appropriate amount when shipping glass and china. This type of item is heavy and requires a great deal of packing material to prevent damage during shipping.

Rating Guideline for Crystal and Glass

Good:

Anchor Hocking
Blenko
Boda
Carnival
Depression Glass
Duncan & Miller
Fenton
Fostoria
Goebal
Godinger

Heisey
Imperial
Lenox
Murano
Neiman Marcus
Northwood
Princess House
Westmoreland

Better:

Cambridge
Gorham
Moser
Orrefors
Pairpoint
Swarovski
Tiffin

BEST:

Baccarat
Dale Chihuly
Daum (Nancy, France)
Galle
Lalique
Loetz
Stueben
Tiffany

ELECTRONIC EQUIPMENT

The key factor to consider when purchasing electronics for resale is depreciation. Depreciation occurs when an item looses value due to use, age, and/or technology changes.

Let's use music as an example. Record albums in various forms were the first device used to record and play music. With minor changes, records remained the main form of music play until 8-track tapes were introduced in the 1970s. This technology allowed music to be played in a mobile setting such as a car, but the quality was not as good as the album, so albums stayed around. The 8-track was quickly replaced by the much better sounding cassette tape. Technology changed again, and now CD players are in almost every home and new car. We are again on the verge of a change. MP3 players allow people to download songs of their choice with high-quality sound. It is just a matter of time before the CD will be as old fashioned as the 8-track tape.

As new technology replaces old, the items associated with the old technology lose value. Record players, 8-track tape players, and cassette players hold very little value except as collector's items for the enthusiast. Certain brands and models can still command good prices because of the die-hard collector, but the mainstream population has moved on.

> Moneymaking tip: If possible, ask to test electronic equipment before purchasing it. If that is not possible, be sure to ask pointed question about the equipment's condition.

Asking the right questions can usually bring out the condition of the electronic equipment you are considering purchasing. But there are occasions when sellers will misrepresent an item or will just not know if it works because it has not been used in a long time. Pay very little or pass up these items.

While it is best to resell electronic and technology-related items as soon as possible due to the ever-changing marketplace, there are some exceptions.

One Man's Trash

> A customer brought in an original Apple computer. This computer was one of the first computers Apple sold to the general public. Our customer had retrieved the computer from his neighbor's trash. The computer was in rough condition, but we were still able to sell it for over $400. This computer sold

for a very good price, because it was one of the first in an industry. Its technology was completely out of date and almost useless, but its value had started to increase after thirty years because it had changed from a piece of technology to a collectible. This is a rare example; most thirty-year-old, technology-related items have very little value.

On your search you will be much more likely to find electronics that are a few years old but still in good condition. There are many people who like to continuously upgrade their electronics. They want to have the latest gadgets so they discard their old electronics frequently. Most of these electronics are in very good condition and have a lot of life left in them. These types of items are all over the marketplace, and huge profits can be made if you look for quality. Electronic companies are always updating their products so this is a good area to find items for resale.

Moneymaking tip: If you plan to make reselling electronics your main focus, you will want to keep updated on the trends and the marketplace. Look at the sales ads and price records or online auctions. Visit retail electronic stores to keep current on the technology.

Rating Guideline for Electronic Equipment

(brand-name ratings cover computers, cameras, audio equipment, and video equipment)

Good:

Emerson
Fisher
JVC
Kenwood
RCA
Sanyo
Sharp
Symphonic
Teac
Zenith

Better:

Akai
Alpine
Auto Research
Blaupunkt
Bose (some best models)
Clarion
Denon
LG Electronics (Life's Good)
Marantz
NAD
Nakamichi
Onkyo
Panasonic (some good and best models)
Philips
Pioneer (some good and best models)
Proton
Sansui
Sony (some good and best models)
Technics
YAMAHA (some good and best models)

Best:

Accuphase
Adcom
Audio Research
Bang & Olufsen
Bose
B & W
Carver
Harmon Kardon
Kimber Kables
Klipsch
Krell
McCormack
McIntosh
Pioneer (high-end models)

Polk
Sony (high-end models)

Housewares: Linens, Flatware, Pet Supplies, Lamps, and More

You will find a great deal of housewares at yard sales and flea markets, but be cautious when purchasing these items. As a general rule, used housewares do not sell for high-dollar amounts online. If you are looking to resell these items, search for *expensive brand-name items* that are in unused—still new, in-the-box—condition. Many people get these items as gifts and never use them, so you can find housewares at yard sales that are new and still in the box. Keep in mind the original retail price of such items. There are many kitchen appliances that retail for several hundred dollars. Those are the type of items you want to seek out, not the $20 can opener. Also, keep in mind the weight of the item. Some kitchen appliances can weigh ten to fifteen pounds and, thus, can be expensive to ship. A buyer will factor in the shipping cost when determining his or her bid.

There are many expensive household items that can be found at inexpensive prices. Keep in mind that you will be competing with many wholesalers in this category, so you need to be able to buy these items cheaply. There are many people who look to online auctions to purchase everyday flatware (sterling flatware is discussed in the section on metalware), pet supplies, dinnerware, glassware, bed linens, and more so you have a market, but you must buy brand names. The brand name is the most important factor in this and the clothing category, so stay away from unknown or box store names. Most local auctions will not take everyday household items so online may be your only place to resell these goods.

> Moneymaking tip: Always consider the original purchase price of an item. Most items sell for less than 50 percent of their original retail price.

Rating Guideline for Housewares

(fine china ratings listed under China; sterling flatware ratings listed under Metalware)

Good:

Berghoff
Calphalon
Chris Madden
Corning

Croscill Spa
Cuisinart
DeLonghi
Faberware
Kenmore
Orbit
Oscar
Pacific Coast
Pottery Barn
Saladmaster
Sharp
Whirlpool
Williams Sonoma

Better:

Arcadia
Bosch
Bowhaus
Calvin Klein
Dualit
Gaggia
Innotek
Jenn-Air
KitchenAid
Le Creuset
La Pavoni
Laura Ashley
Marrikas
Petsafe
Prestige
Ralph Lauren (some best)
Saeco
Tommy Hilfiger
Townecraft
Vita-Mix

Best:

All Clad
Jura
Norwalk
Ralph Lauren (some better)
Ruffoni
Versace
Viking

JEWELRY

Both fine and costume jewelry can be found at prices that are affordable for resale. Fine jewelry is defined by pieces made of precious metals such as gold or silver and/or with precious or semi precious gemstones. Almost all jewelry made of gold or silver will be stamped with the gold or silver content in the piece. See the list of jewelry terms below for more information on the marks found on jewelry.

Common Marks found on Jewelry

Plat. Setting is made of platinum.

18kt. Setting is made of eighteen-karat gold.

14kt. Setting is made of fourteen-karat gold. This is the U.S. standard for most jewelry.

10kt. Setting is made of ten-karat gold. As a general rule, jewelry made of this gold standard is of lesser quality, and any gemstones within this setting can be of lesser quality or simulated stones.

9kt. Setting is made of nine-karat gold. This mark is most likely found on jewelry made in European countries.

333. A reference to the percentage of a setting's gold content that is the equivalent of eight-karat gold. It is usually found on jewelry of European or Asian origin.

417. A reference to the percentage of gold content that is the equivalent of ten-karat gold. It is usually found on jewelry of European or Asian origin.

583 or 585. A reference to the percentage of gold content that is the equivalent of fourteen-karat gold. It is usually found on jewelry of European or Asian origin.

750. A reference to the percentage of gold content that is the equivalent of eighteen-karat gold. It is usually found on jewelry of European or Asian origin.

GP. Likely an abbreviation for the term *gold plum* (not to be confused with gold plated). Jewelry made from gold plum is virtually the same as regular gold that is its equal in karat weight. The gold content will precede this mark for example 14kt or 10kt.

GE. An abbreviation for gold electroplate. In jewelry marked GE, gold has been electroplated, or covered, onto another metal; electroplating is an inexpensive way to get the look of real gold without the expense. The gold content will precede this mark for example 14kt or 10kt.

H.G.E. An abbreviation for heavy gold electroplate. In jewelry marked H.G.E., a heavier layer of gold has been electroplated, or covered, onto another metal than that used in jewelry marked GE, in order to make the piece wear better and longer. The gold content will precede this mark for example 14kt or 10kt.

925 or sterling. An indication that the piece is made from sterling silver. In the United States and most other countries, an item must be made of at least 925/1000 parts silver to other metals to be considered sterling silver.

830. A marking found on some silver jewelry that indicates that the piece is made from 830/1000 parts silver to other metals. This mark is found on some vintage and foreign pieces.

gold over sterling. A mark that indicates that the piece is made from sterling and has a thin layer of gold over the sterling. The gold content most likely will precede this mark.

Jewelry Terms to Know

amber. Fossilized resin from trees. Tiny leaves or insects can sometimes be found inside a polished piece of amber. Amber is s now being artificially created in plastics.

aurora borealis. An iridescent coating applied to faceted glass beads or rhinestones to give them extra shininess and sparkle. The technique was developed by Swarovski Corporation in 1955.

baguette. A narrow rectangular faceted stone.

bakelite. The first fully synthetic resin/plastic. Leo Baekeland developed bakelite in 1909. Bakelite is used in many jewelry items. It can be made to simulate ivory, tortoise shell, and other natural materials and is very collectible.

bangle. A rigid circular bracelet.

bog oak. Fossilized peat found mainly in nineteenth-century carved Irish jewelry and made popular by Queen Elizabeth I.

brilliant. The name of the circular cut for gemstones with 58 facets.

cabochon. An un-faceted, domed cut with a flat base used for gemstones or glass stones.

cameo. A design carved in relief often from shell or stone but now being imitated in plastics. Usually the carving is of a beautiful woman or floral designs. Scenic views are rarer and thus more desirable.

carat. A unit of weight for gemstones.

Celluloid. The trade name for semi-synthetic thermoplastic that was invented by John Wesley Hyatt in 1868. Celluloid is highly collectible.

choker. A necklace that fits snuggly around the neck.

circa. Within ten years of the given date.

cloisonné. An enameling technique in which tiny wires are placed on an object to form a design and the spaces around the wires are filled in with enamel. The technique is used on jewelry and pottery.

costume jewelry. Jewelry that is made from non precious metals and stones.

culet. A small, flat bottom cut found on older cut stones.

cultured pearl. A pearl produced by inserting an irritant into an oyster or other mollusk. A natural pearl is formed when the irritant is introduced by nature.

electroplate. The electrolytic process of applying one metal over another, most often gold over a base metal.

facet. The plane cut of a stone.

faux. A French term meaning fake or false.

filigree. A decoration on jewelry that is usually made with thin wires to form an ornate setting.

fine jewelry. Jewelry made from precious metals and/or stones.

foiled back. A process where a very thin layer of metal is applied—sometimes painted—on the backs of stones, usually rhinestones, to enhance the look of the stones.

gold-filled/gold-plated. When a layer of gold is applied to a base metal. The U. S. standard is that gold has to comprise at least 1/20th of a piece's total weight in order for it to be marked gold-filled. The percentage of gold in a piece marked gold-plated is often less, and the marking usually indicates that the electroplate technique has been used.

graduated. An arrangement, usually of beads or pearls, that is ascending or descending in order. Usually the smaller beads in the back of the necklace arrive at the largest bead in the front center.

hair jewelry. Jewelry or pieces made with human hair. Popular during the Victorian era, hair jewelry is very collectable today.

hallmark. The mark or marks stamped on metal indicating the fineness of the metal. Hallmarks can also indicate the maker and/or origin of the piece.

karat. An indication of the fineness of the gold alloy of a piece. Twenty-four-karat (24kt) gold is pure gold.

Lucite. The trade name of a plastic used to create some jewelry pieces.

marcasite. Iron pyrite with silvery black tones used in jewelry to create a shiny look. Maracasite is often used in silver jewelry and with onyx stones.

marquise cut. A gemstone with an oval cut with pointed ends. The cut is most often associated with diamonds.

Moissanite. A trade name for a synthetic diamond that is chemically, physically, and optically identical to a diamond in every way. Moissanite will test as a true diamond on most standard diamond testers. Moissanite testers are now available on the marketplace.

mother-of-pearl. The pearl-like lining of a mollusk, which is used in jewelry making.

mourning jewelry. Jewelry worn, mostly by women, to remember a loved one who has died. Often black, mourning jewelry sometimes contains a picture of a person or a lock of the loved one's hair. This type of jewelry was most popular during the Victorian era.

old European cut. A brilliant cut for diamonds with fewer facets or cuts. This cut is no longer used today.

old mine cut. A brilliant cut for diamonds with fewer facets or cuts but with more of a cushion-shaped stone and large culet. This cut is no longer used today.

pave. A method of setting small stones very close together, such as in a paved stone walkway.

prong setting. The method of setting stones with metal prongs.

provenance. The origin or history of the piece.

relief. The raised design or raised area of a piece. When you touch an object that has relief, you can detect a difference in the levels; the piece's surface is not flat.

rhinestone. The first faux diamond. Original rhinestones came from the area near the Rhine River. The term now refers to any vintage cut glass stones in costume jewelry.

rock crystal. Clear quartz stone used in costume jewelry.

rose gold. Gold that is mixed with copper, giving it a more pinkish appearance than normal gold.

scarab. An Egyptian term for beetle. Scarab symbols were carved into stones or glass and made into jewelry.

seed pearl. A tiny pearl, natural or cultured, weighing less than one gram. Seed pearls were used in a lot of Victorian-era jewelry.

slave bracelet. A bangle bracelet worn on the upper arm, which was first popular in the 1920s.

slide. A moveable pendant worn with a chain necklace or bracelet. The piece has a hole in the center and will "slide" over the chain.

solitaire. A single gemstone—usually diamond engagement rings—mounted in a setting.

sterling silver. Silver that is comprised of 925: 1000 parts silver to other metals. Sterling silver is commonly used in jewelry making, both past and present.

synthetic gemstone. A laboratory-created gemstone that is chemically, physically, and optically identical to its natural counterpart.

vulcanite. A vulcanized rubber used for jewelry making in the nineteenth century, which is also known as Ebonite.

white gold. An alloy of gold that contains nickel, palladium, or platinum, producing a silver-colored gold.

A Word About Gemstones

Simulated gemstones have been in the marketplace since the early nineteenth century. In today's marketplace, simulated gemstones are made so well they can sometimes fool even experienced jewelers. The simulated diamond Moissanite is a manmade diamond, and only an electronic Moissanite tester can distinguish a real diamond from a Moissanite. So when buying jewelry, be very cautious, especially if you do not know the person or company from whom you are buying. Make sure you have a written, detailed description of the piece that includes the carat weight of any stones and the gold content. A reputable auctioneer or online seller should be willing to guarantee in writing any jewelry you purchase. We also recommend that you immediately take any jewelry you purchase to a trusted jeweler for verification and an appraisal.

As we have mentioned before, designer name will add value to jewelry sold online. It does not matter if the piece is vintage or currently produced, items carrying a designer name will sell better online than no-name items. If you plan to concentrate your resale efforts in the jewelry market, you will want to invest in several quality jewelry books with jewelry-maker hallmarks listed for reference. We have listed some of the most popular fine jewelry makers' names below.

Rating Guideline for Fine Jewelry Makers

Good:

Brighton
James Avery
Judith Jack
Lori Bonn
Michael Dawkins

Better:

Gucci
Hermes
John Hardy
Judith Ripka
Lagos
Mikimoto (pearls)
Roberto Coin
Stephen Dweck

Best:

Bulgari
Cartier
Chanel
Chopard
David Yurman
Georg Jensen
Tiffany

Costume Jewelry

Quality costume jewelry is extremely collectible and affordable. The best return on costume jewelry is in the vintage market. You can resell the recently made costume jewelry, but know your price points. Remember that modern-made costume jewelry only commands pennies on the dollar in the resale market. Collectors are especially attracted to designer names and fancy or unusual pieces. Look for pieces that are pretty, ornate, and have matching pieces. Condition is extremely important. Check to make sure that there are no missing stones and the rhinestones are clear and bright, not foggy. Also check the setting of the piece for damage and discoloration. You will find that many of the vintage pieces are dirty or dingy. If you decide to clean the pieces, make sure you perform the function properly. Moisture will turn rhinestones dark and cloudy. There are several websites that provide detailed instructions on the cleaning of rhinestones and vintage jewelry.

Gold Glitters but Rhinestones Shine

One of our favorite customers brought in a blue rhinestone floral brooch by Miriam Haskell. This great vintage piece had everything going for it. It was lovely, large, in perfect condition, and by a known and collected designer. We sold the piece online for $360. This Haskell brooch was made of mere rhinestones and metal not gold or gemstones, yet it sold for more money than many average brooches made of silver and gold. Always remember the basic Flipster philosophy that quality always sells.

Rating Guidelines for Costume Jewelry Makers

Good:

Banana Republic
Brighton
Carolee
Coro
Guess
Joan Rivers
Juicy Couture
Michal Negrin (mainly crystal pieces)
Sarah Coventry
Trifari

Better:

Juliana Dangling
Kenneth J. Lane
Kirks Folly
Lisner
Liz Palacios
Nolan Miller
Originals By Robert
Sorrelli
Weiss
Winard (Many items made in gold plate)

Best:

Cari
Eisenberg
Hattie Carnegie (signed "Carnegie")
Marcel Boucher
Miriam Haskell
Schiaparelli
Schreiner

MEDIA ITEMS: BOOKS, VIDEOS, DVDs, CDs AND RECORDS

The media category is an odd one. We cannot possibly list all the millions of titles you will come in contact with on your search, so we have instead opted to give you a set of guidelines that will direct you to those purchases that will help you reap the most return for your investment dollar.

The great thing about books and DVDs is you can sell them on Amazon.com as well as the online auction sites. When you sell on Amazon.com, you just set your price, and the item stays available on the site until it sells for that price. You want to price it competitively so it sells quickly. Amazon takes care of receiving the payment from the buyer and will notify you when and where to ship the media item. Listing your item is free on Amazon, but the site does take a small percentage if your item sells.

It is easy to register and to list your items on Amazon. There is no need to take a picture of the book or media item; you can list it by its International Standard Book Number (ISBN). Almost all books or media items made within the last thirty years have an ISBN. The ISBN is located on the back of the product or inside the book on the same page as the copyright information. For more information about selling your books, videos, and DVDs go to www.amazon.com.

VHS and Cassettes

Do not waste your time or money on VHS videos or cassettes. This is a dying technology, and it will soon become obsolete. The only exception to this rule would be strange, odd, or rare videos that may still be of value or complete collections or sets.

Books

Any book that was a bestseller and therefore sold millions of copies should be avoided. Although one might think very popular books would sell well, this is a simple example of how supply and demand works. There are just too many used bestselling books on the marketplace. For example, a used copy of the 1992 best selling novel *The Firm* by John Grisham is at the time of this printing selling for less than $1 on Amazon.com. However, the 1984 book *Coconut Grove* by Edward Keyes, which is about the 1942 tragic fire at Boston's Coconut Grove and was much less popular at the time of its printing, now sells for over $200 on the web. Keyes's book about the Coconut Grove came to be an important book regarding a historical event *after the printing had ended*, so this book is rare and has become a collector's item.

Some first-edition books can sell for huge prices online, but many first-edition books get very little. So before you spend hundreds of dollars for a first-edition book, be sure to do your homework. There are also levels of "first editions." There are first editions, first printings, which are the most valuable, but there are first editions with later printings, sometimes twentieth or thirtieth printings, which are much less prized by collectors. Be sure to read carefully all the information on the publishing page before you purchase. Rare-book buying is an intricate business, and you should gain knowledge and experience before investing too much of your capital in this area.

Another area we would like to mention is vintage and antique books. Just because a book is very old does not make it valuable. I have seen books that were over one hundred years old that held little to no value in the marketplace. Many of these books were in very poor condition, which of course decreases their value greatly. If the love of books is your passion, I suggest you work and study with a local antiquarian before you venture out and try to buy and resell antique books on your own. Anything and everything can affect the value of the book—from its printing, to its publisher, to the way it was bound. This is a wonderful and noble business, but it requires special knowledge that I cannot bring to you in this field guide.

DVDs and CDs

Purchasing DVDs and CDs can be a mixed bag. If you can get them extremely cheap, then they may be worth your time. Keep in mind that there are many people selling DVDs on online auction sites. You will have a lot of competition. Also keep in mind that DVDs and CDs are already *old* technology; in the near future, no one will want to purchase them.

In this area, block buster movies or CDs that are hot can sell, but unique and collectible items may be better. The third rate "B" movies or CDs that performed poorly when released would be the least desirable.

Instructional Media

There are certain instructional media sold in sets or collections that can be very valuable on the online auctions sites. Many of these items are business-related or "how to" instructional media. Either weight loss or sports is often the subject matter of these package sets. Try to find the original retail price of the item. Some of these sets originally sold for several hundred dollars, but some sold for as low as $20. That is your first decision point. If the original sales price of an item was $20, the resale is likely to be less than $5, so pass it up.

Also, look at the name attached to the item. Is it a person or a company you recognize? If the media item had a retail sales price of $300 and has been released by a respected person in the related field, then chances are the resale price of the item will be good. A great example is the Hooked on Phonics system. The retail price for these sets, depending on the version of the set, is anywhere from $200 to $400. Sets sell on eBay for between $100 and $200. If you can purchase a set in like-new condition for $10 to $40, you most likely have a winning purchase. The caution here is to make sure the item is in great condition and not so old that several new versions are on the marketplace.

Old car manuals and electronic equipment manuals can be another source of great moneymaking. People restore vintage cars and need the old manuals to help in the restoring process. Other people just like to collect car manuals. Some manuals will sell for hundreds of dollars on eBay.

Records

There are only a handful of diehard record collectors left to buy old record albums so there is no mass market appeal. Just as with most areas, there are a few very valuable records floating around in the marketplace, but finding those records will be very unlikely. My advice is to leave the record albums on the table and move on to something that is more likely to be profitable.

Moneymaking tip: Phone a friend to lower your risk. Have someone waiting at home to check on items that you think, but aren't sure, will be real moneymakers. A quick search of the item's ISBN at Amazon's website will reveal the current going rate for any book that is less than thirty years old. For older books, search the title and the author.

This technique has worked well for Daren and me. I will go down to the thrift store and pick out books I think may have a potential to make money. I'll choose business books or instructional books. Then I'll gather all the potential purchases and read off the ISBNs to Daren over the phone. Most books at this type of store are priced at fifty cents to $1, so they're an inexpensive investment. (I do not purchase books unless they will sell for at least $25 online. I want to make sure my investments are worth the time it takes to resell the item.) I'll always come home with at least three books and sometimes many more. We have had several books sell for $200 or more online.

METALWARE: BRASS, BRONZE, COPPER AND SILVER

Brass:

For the most part, brass is currently out of favor with collectors, but there are some exceptions such as when the artistic value of the piece outweighs the fact that the piece is made of brass. Look for unique sculptures, nice old hardware, and hand-hammered items. Avoid any brass items that are marked "India."

Bronze:

When one thinks of bronze, one usually conjures images of beautiful, old bronze statues, which are still highly collectible and worth a considerable amount of money. However, just like many other things, there are bronze statues being reproduced today that are of extremely poor quality and not worth very much on the open market. There are also statues and sculptures that have been and are currently being produced in white metal that is then covered in bronze. The modern-made versions of these statues will, again, be poor quality and worth very little. The antique versions of these bronze-over-metal statues, while not as valuable as true bronzes, can be valuable pieces. The key here is to look for quality. Look at the construction and the details of the piece. Antique bronze bookends are great pieces to consider when shopping.

Copper:

During the Arts and Crafts movement, copper was used to create useful and decorative household items such as bookends, bowls, and ashtrays. Items made during this period were handmade and of high artistic quality. These are the types of copper items you should seek out. Unfortunately, you are more likely to encounter a great deal of pressed copper plates, knickknacks, and little figures, most of which are not worth very much.

Sterling Silver and Silver Plate:

Sterling silver is solid silver made up of 925/1000 parts silver to other metal. If you were to cut a piece of sterling silver down the middle, the interior of the piece would look the same as the exterior of the piece. The term *silver plate* refers to a process where a thin layer of sterling is applied over another metal, usually brass, copper, or white metal. If you were to cut a piece of silver plate down the middle, you would be able to see a thin layer of silver surrounding a thick base metal. Silver plate can be marked "plate" or "EP" which stands for electroplate. Electroplate is the process used to adhere the silver to the metal. Sterling can be marked "925" or "sterling." Sometimes the piece is not marked at all or the mark has been polished away. As a general rule, sterling silver is much more valuable than silver plate, but that is not always the case. Older silver is almost always a better quality than newly made silver items and thus the older silver is more valuable.

There are thousands of hallmarks dating back hundreds of years from all countries. If you are going to specialize in silver items, you will need to purchase a silver hallmarks book so you can correctly identify the manufacturer. You will also want to purchase at least one book on flatware pattern identification. Below I will list some of the most popular American silver manufacturers, but some of the most valuable silver was made in other countries. So be aware that, if you only look for American silver, you are limiting your profit potential.

Most of the silver you will encounter, besides jewelry, will be flatware and hollowware. The resale price of these goods will depend as much on the pattern of the pieces as the manufacturer's name. There are thousands of pattern names, so I cannot rank them all, but as a general rule, the more ornate the pattern, the more expensive the item.

Also keep in mind that almost all major sterling manufactures produced silver-plated items too. So be sure to look at all the hallmarks on the back of the piece to determine if the item is sterling or silver plate.

Rating Guideline for Metalware

Good:

1847 Rogers (silver plate)
Alvin Sterling
Baldwin Brass
Brass Bookends
Brass Sculptures
F. B. Rogers (silver plate)
Lunt Sterling
Manchester Sterling

Oneida Sterling
Remington (some better)
Watson Sterling
Webster Sterling
Whiting & Davis Sterling
Whiting, Frank Sterling
Wm. Rogers

Better:

Barbour (silver plate)
Black, Star & Frost
Black, Star & Gorham
Durgin Sterling
ETC Fish
Gorham (some best)
Hagenauer
Heintz
Hubley
International Sterling
Kirk & Son or S. Kirk & Son Sterling
Kirk Steiff Company Sterling
Loet
Reed and Barton Sterling
Remington statues and sculptures (some good)
Rena Rosenthal
Samovar
Sheffield Silver (plate)
Tim Cotterill
Towle Sterling
Wallace Sterling
Williamsburg

Best:

Antique brass hardware (*not* modern reproductions)
Bradley & Hubbard
Bronze Bookends
Bronze Sculptures
Christofle

Dominick and Haff
Georg Jensen
Gorham (some better)
Roycroft
Stickley
Tiffany
Unger Brothers Sterling
Walter Von Nessen

Gold Mine:

Tiffany–Chrysanthemum pattern
Gorham–Narragansett pattern
Reed & Barton–Love Disarmed

MUSICAL INSTRUMENTS

Almost all musical instruments are expensive to purchase new so the resale value can be significant. Most of the musical instruments you will encounter will be average, student/beginner-type instruments. Most of these come from parents seeking to rid themselves of unused instruments after a child has abandoned the pursuit. However, if you do find professional grade, vintage, or even antique instruments, they can command extremely high prices.

You are usually able to identify vintage or antique instrument by the material they are made from and the quality of the construction. High-quality instruments do not have plastic pieces, and the workmanship is generally handcrafted. The case of a quality instrument should be made of wood or leather.

The Tell-Tale Case

Daren found a great old instrument on one of his buying trips. The seller was asking $35 for an oboe that he had found in his family home. He had no information about the piece or who may have used it. Daren examined the instrument and noticed that it had a fine-tooled leather case and was hand-constructed of a unique, dark wood. These two factors were dead giveaways that this instrument was something of value. More expensive instruments are housed in ornate boxes, and this oboe case was made of lovely ebony. Based on that information, Daren was willing to take a risk and purchase the oboe. I researched the piece and discovered that it had been made by a well-known manufacturer, and it was a rare and desirable piece. I was able to sell the oboe for over $450. This example is meant to show you how to look for clues that point to quality, uniqueness, and desirability. You do not have to be an expert in the musical instrument field to find what will sell.

Most student instruments are made of lower-quality materials such as low-quality plastics, metal, or wood. Carefully examine each piece you consider buying, looking at the construction, the detail, and the craftsmanship. Do the pieces fit together tightly and smoothly? Is there detailed workmanship to the piece? Does it have mother-of-pearl or ivory inlay? Is it carved, handmade, or machine made? Is the piece made from high-quality or exotic materials such as ebony, tiger maple, or burl wood? Consider the country of origin. Modern day instruments imported from China or India are most likely a lower-quality item. Another clue to determining the quality of an instrument is the quality of the case. Leather or nice wooden cases with high-quality silk or velvet interiors are usually a good indicator of a quality instrument. Accessories that are found in the case can add to the resale value of the piece.

One more thing to consider when purchasing musical instruments for resale is the popularity of an instrument. When you are reselling any item, you want to appeal to the widest possible market. We have found that all levels of guitars seem to sell well. However, when we tried to sell a cello, we had to try several selling avenues in order to find a buyer. After four weeks and a short cello recital in our offices, it finally sold. There are a lot more guitar players than there are cello players in my area, but the other problem with the cello was its size. It is easy to pack up a violin or guitar for shipping, but it is much harder and more expensive to try and ship a cello. Always keep shipping constraints in the back of your mind when you're looking for items to sell.

Sweet Music Saved from Trash

We had a gentleman bring in a violin that he was about to *throw in the trash*, but he wanted to get our opinion first. Thank goodness he did!

We examined the violin and saw that it did need repair, and the case was falling apart. The violin was dirty, the bridge was cracked, and the bow was in poor shape. However, the body was made of beautiful, flamed tiger maple, and it appeared to be very well made. We decided it was worth the time to research the maker. We found that the violin was over one hundred years old and was made by a well-known violin maker in Germany. Even with all the condition issues, the violin sold for well over $1000. The owner was shocked and obviously very happy that he had stopped by eBizAuctions before making a stop at the trash bin.

PHOTOGRAPHY EQUIPMENT

Photography equipment has a high secondary-market value. Many people like to upgrade or change their current equipment, so there are a lot of photography items circulating in the marketplace. Photographic and optical equipment that is worth selling can range from antiques to the latest digital models or classic 35 mm cameras. Cameras, Camcorders, lenses, telescopes, binoculars, and accessories can have high resale values.

Photography equipment can be highly sensitive equipment with many parts and attachments. If not properly cared for and stored, these items can be easily damaged. We highly recommend that you take some time in examining each piece and if possible test the equipment before you make a purchase. Some of the types you will encounter are listed below.

Single Lens Reflex (SLR) Cameras

The SLR cameras are a popular choice, because they offer versatility. Most SLR cameras feature interchangeable lenses and an extensive accessory system that lets the user handle any task.

35 mm Compact Cameras

These cameras are easy to use, but they have limited abilities. They nearly all have just a single lens, which requires the subject to be at least four feet away. Most also include a built-in flash and auto exposure.

Instant-print Cameras

These cameras are only available now from Polaroid, and Polaroid also makes the film. These cameras produce color or black-and-white photos within seconds of taking the picture, so this unique feature will continue to make them popular.

Digital Cameras

The future of photography is in the digital camera. No longer is film needed, and the prices of digital cameras have dropped in recent years, so they are affordable to just about anyone. The image is recorded on a disk or memory stick. This medium can then be used to transfer images to print or to the web or just about anywhere.

The one thing to consider with digital cameras is the mega pixels. The more mega pixels you have, the clearer and sharper your image will be. Anywhere from a three- to six-mega pixel camera is considered to be a good choice. Generally speaking, the higher the mega pixels, the more costly the camera. Of course to work with digital cameras, you will need the appropriate software and printer, which are accessories buyers will also be looking to purchase.

Our rating system below gives a general overview of manufacturers, but every manufacturer has both lower-end and higher-end models. The resale price difference varies greatly depending upon the model, condition, and whether there are any accessories that go with the camera. Also, some lenses are worth more than the cameras, so do not be afraid to purchase just a lens or camera accessory.

Lenses

There is a wide variety of lenses on the secondary market, and many lenses will command higher prices than many cameras. Look for specialty lenses with great brand names.

Antique and Vintage Equipment

Do not forget about great antique and vintage camera-related items. These items can be very good moneymakers. You will come in contact with opera glasses, stereo cameras, View-Masters, and more. Try to find the rare and unusual items. Look for items made with expensive materials and those that have quality construction.

Rating Guideline for Photography Equipment

Good:

Bell and Howell
Fuji (some better)
Kodak
Polaroid
Yashika

Better:

Cannon
Contax
Fuji
Konica
Leica
Minolta
Minox
Olympus
Panasonic (some best)
Pentax
Ricoh
Sony (some best)
Vivitar
Ziess (camera)

Best:

Hasselblad
Leica
Mamiya (some better)
Nikon
Ziess (lenses)

POTTERY AND ART POTTERY

The Battle for the Panel Vase

One of my regular customers brought in a Brush McCoy vase for me to sell. Normally Brush McCoy items do not generate a great deal of excitement on eBay, but this one was special. This Brush McCoy vase was from the panel art series, and the Collector's Encyclopedia of Brush–McCoy Pottery stated that the value was between $600 and $800. Now we both knew the stated values listed in the books have very little to do with the actual price you will receive for your item. Ninety-nine percent of the time, the book value will be much more than the actual value you will receive at auction. This vase fell into the one percent category.

My customer stated that he would be happy with a final price of $400 on the piece, so we started it a little lower. During the week, bids for the vase slowly climbed to around $600, and we were both very happy, thinking that would be the final price.

We were so wrong! In the final two minutes of the auction, the bids climbed to over $1,700. It was like pulling the arm down on a Las Vegas slot machine and hearing the money fall. We could not believe that the vase had sold for over twice as much as the book value.

After the auction ended, I had to contact the buyer and ask him why he was willing to pay so much for this vase, which experts deemed worth only $800. The buyer told me that he did not care what the piece's book value was. He had a hole in his collection, and these vases are very hard to find, so he was going to have it. This auction was great for him, great for my customer, and great for me.

Pottery is one of my favorite things. It can be made into just about any shape, form, or design. Art pottery can be found to fit any décor or design while also being utilitarian. It is easy to find a piece of art pottery you love, but it is much harder to determine the value of a piece just by its mark or name. All the major pottery makers have different lines and prices that vary greatly depending on the item. The Brush McCoy case is great example of the deviation in price that one producer can have in its line. The average sales price for Brush McCoy items is around $35, yet we sold one vase for over $1,700.

So how does one purchase art pottery without risk? If possible, do your research before you buy. The rating guide below is based on the *average selling price online for the maker*. Use the guide as a first step to help you make a smart purchase.

Some other important factors to look for when purchasing art pottery are detail, scale, and condition. If a piece has detailed form or detailed hand-painted scenes, then it may be a piece with higher value. Larger pieces of art pottery are rarer, so therefore they are usually more expensive. Larger pieces are harder to make, so not as many were produced. Also, larger pieces tend to get broken more often than smaller pieces. Smaller pieces can be stored behind glass in a china cabinet and, thus, protected against damage. We have talked about condition at length throughout this book, but I would like to emphasize it again. It is much easier to repair pottery pieces than other types of art, so be sure to look for repairs, and ask the owner if there has ever been a repair to the piece.

Avoid purchasing mass-produced, modern-day pottery pieces that can be found in every strip mall franchise store across the country. These will not sell well online or at auction. If the piece has a tag the reads "made in China," leave it on the table.

Rating Guideline for Art Pottery

Good:

Brush McCoy
Capodimonte
Colorado Pottery
Coors Pottery
Dakota Pottery
Frankoma (some better)
Hadley (some better)
Haeger (some better)
Hull
McCoy
North Carolina Pottery (general)
Robinson Ransbottom
Rosemeade
Stangl
Van Briggle

Better:

Clarice Cliff
Coalport

Cole, JB (North Carolina potter)
Craig (North Carolina potter)
Fulper (some best)
Gouda
Hussey, Billy Ray
Newcomb
Owen, Ben
Pisgah Forest
Poole
Quimper
Roseville

Best:

Beswick
Clarice Cliff
Greuby
Moorcroft
North Carolina Face Jug Pottery
Rookwood
Royal Vienna
Teco
Weller (some better)

SPORTING GOODS

The sporting goods industry is a multimillion-dollar industry encompassing everything from athletic footwear to collectibles memorabilia. Many people have heard about certain baseball cards receiving thousands or millions of dollars at auction, but it is unlikely that you are going to find rare and valuable baseball cards on a regular basis. If you happen to run across someone selling a mint condition 1918 Babe Ruth baseball card for $20 dollars, we do not need to tell you to buy it. You already know that. Keep in mind that the old cards are currently being reproduced. Most of these reproduced cards will state the year they were produced, but be sure to check.

The information in this section will inform you about the average new and used sporting goods equipment and related paraphernalia. There are hundreds of millions of people actively involved in sports and hundreds of millions more who want to be or have just given up a sport. That is to say, it is an ever-changing sports world, and you can cash in on it. Some people are just getting into a sport so they want new gear. Others are getting out of a sport so they want to sell their gear. Kids outgrow their equipment, and adults get bored with theirs. Some buy things they never used, and others use their equipment only once or twice, so it is like new.

As with everything else, look for great condition and expensive items. The big exception to this rule is the exercise machine. Unless you have a storefront or a big storage space, do not waste your time on large treadmills, step machines, and so forth. They are impossible to ship, heavy and bulky to move, and the resale value is usually less than a quarter of the retail sale price. Try to focus on the smaller items. New items are great, but there is also a huge market for vintage sporting goods.

Runaway Bids for Old Sneakers

You would likely think that used athletic shoes would not have a high resale value, but you would be wrong. When we first started selling items on eBay, Daren pulled out a pair of his old, black Nike high-top sneakers to sell. I never would have believed that anyone would want a pair of old shoes, but someone did. These shoes were in very good condition, because Daren only wore them a few times before they got pushed to the back of the closet and forgotten about. We were both amazed that these shoes were purchased for over $100 on eBay. We later sold another pair of vintage skate shoes for over $50. It is amazing what people will purchase online.

Rating Guideline for Sporting Goods

Good:

Coleman
L.L. Bean
Louisville
Nike (some better)
Oakley
Patagonia
Rawlings
Remington
Spalding
Tasco
Wilson

Better:

Adidas
Burton
Callaway
DeMarini
Elan
Everlast
K2
Nike (some good)
The North Face
Penn Senator
Salomon
Schwinn (some best)
Shimano
Titlest

Best:

Bushnell
Elan

Leupold
Mizuno
Ping
Schwinn (some better)
Taylor Made
Titlest
Trek

TOYS, DOLLS AND PLUSH ANIMALS

The Forgotten Christmas Gift

This is one of my favorite stories to tell. A woman was cleaning out her attic and came across a Disney Mickey Mouse Weebles Wobble play set from the late 1960s, which had never been opened. She told us that she had purchased it for her children as a gift and stored it in the attic to hide it until Christmas, but she had forgotten about it. She found the play set in the back corner of her attic when she was cleaning out to move to a smaller home now that her children were grown. We had to pay her $20 for the play set, but we knew an unopened pristine Disney toy from the 1960s would command a great price online. We sold it for just over $150. The Weebles Wobble made for a nice little profit and an even better story.

Buying collectible toys for the resale market can be lucrative. Toys have always been and continue to be a highly-collected commodity. Two important factors in purchasing toys are condition and the original box. If the condition is very good, and you have the original box, then the value of the piece can increase dramatically. Of course, there are other important factors in determining the value of a toy, such as age, production levels, and rarity.

Determine the age of a toy before you buy it if possible. Toys produced prior to WWI were made of iron and steel, but during WWI metals were used for the war effort, so metal toys became scarce. After WWII, plastic was introduced, and almost all common toys are now made of a plastic material. A toy does not have to be one hundred years old to be valuable. Most toys made prior to the 1970s were made for children. Children played with and destroyed many of the toys or parents discarded the toys after their children became older.

Another very important factor to consider is the production levels of some toys. Everyone remembers the Beanie Baby craze of the 1990s, when people stood in line for "special" Beanie Babies. At the time, a friend stated that he was going to collect Beanie Babies and then sell them to pay for his children's college education. His kids were six and eight at the time. As we all now know, the Beanie Baby lost favor, and the toys can now be found at just about every yard sale for fifty cents each. Collecting Beanie Babies was not the best plan for financing college.

The Beanie Baby story is a great example of the basic principal of supply and demand. Many modern-day toys go through a "hot" phase where supply cannot keep up with the demand, and the toys command huge, inflated prices. We saw the same thing happen with the Cabbage Patch doll and many of the recently released electronic games. This phenomenon happens just about every Christmas. After Christmas is over, the demand goes down, the manufacturer has a chance to produce enough supply, and the price goes back to normal levels. Remember, toys are not made from products that have intrinsic value such as gold, silver, or other marketable goods. Most of the modern-day toys are made from plastic and cloth, so there is no intrinsic value in the pieces. The value is driven by market demands.

Barbie is a classic example of not only market-driven value but also how a toy becomes a collectible. Early Barbie dolls from the 1950s and 60s were manufactured as toys for children. Children played with Barbie, cut her hair, and broke her, and parents tossed her away. So Barbie dolls from that era are much harder to find, especially in mint or even good condition. The early Barbie dolls receive huge prices, sometimes in the thousands of dollars range. Barbie has now become a collector's item. Modern-day Barbie dolls, those produced in the 1980s and beyond, are purchased not only for children but by collectors. They are produced and purchased by the millions.

The collector does not play with Barbie. She is kept in mint condition in her box, ready to resell. But unfortunately for the collectors trying to resell their Barbie dolls, the dolls will never realize any appreciation in value, and collectors will actually see a huge decrease in value. Why? Most modern-day Barbie dolls are produced by the millions, and they are not being "used up" or disposed of, so they remain in the marketplace. In other words, there is more supply than demand. There are thousands of collectors trying to unload their collections at any one time in the online marketplace. Most of these "collectible" Barbie dolls are sold in retail stores for $30 to $50 each. Go online at any major online auction site, and you will see that the same dolls sell for $8 to $15 each or less. This is a sad reality check I have had to give to many Barbie collectors over the years.

So as a general rule, when a toy or any product is being produced by the millions, the value will not increase for a very long time, if at all. Also keep in mind that many of these products are mass-produced with inexpensive materials. They are not fine hand-painted porcelain, hand-blown glass, artist-made pottery, gold, or gemstones. Their value is determined solely by marketing.

The doll market is now depressed, and it has been for many years. Most women today do not collect dolls like many did in the past. Many big doll collectors are older women who are downsizing their collections or have passed away. In the past year, I have helped sell three doll collector's estates, and I have seen many doll auctions across the country. With so many dolls flooding the market and so few collectors, the prices have gone down.

Just because the doll is old does not make it valuable. In fact, there are more recent dolls that are more valuable than the older dolls. I am sure that everyone has heard of Shirley Temple, who became famous as a child movie star in the 1930s and '40s. Many dolls were made in her likeness during the height of her career, and at one time Shirley Temple dolls commanded tremendous prices at auctions. However, there are not many people collecting dolls now who have a personal memory or connection with this star. People who were children during the '30s and '40s are over sixty years old today, so even those who are collectors are most likely not collecting dolls anymore; rather they are probably downsizing their collections. So even though the dolls are getting older, the price of Shirley Temple dolls has gone down, because there are fewer buyers. The older Shirley Temple dolls still command very high prices, but even still, the prices are down compared to what the dolls sold for ten to twenty years ago. Many people collect dolls and toys that they had when they were children, so toys from the 1960s to 1980s are becoming collectibles now.

The Lion with Two Tales

Daren walked into a local thrift store and entered a room that was filled with mostly junky toys. His attention focused on a small stuffed lion. The lion had glass eyes and was made of mohair. Daren checked the lion's ear for the Steiff tag he was expecting, but there was no tag. However, there was the tiny tell-tale hole where the Steiff metal button tag had once been. Daren took the lion home for fifty cents, and a week later, he sold the stuffed animal online for over $50.

That is not the end, nor is it the best part, of this story. The buyer of the vintage lion had his own story. The man said that he had been looking for this old Steiff lion for years to purchase for his wife. He told me that he had accidentally discarded his wife's lion, which she had had since childhood. He wanted badly to replace it and had been searching everywhere to find one. He had just recently started to look on eBay and was amazed to find this old stuffed Steiff lion. It was nice to be able to make a profit, but it was equally nice to replace a childhood memory and get a husband out of the doghouse.

Rating Guidelines for Toys

Good:

American Girl
Boyd Bears
Corgi
Danbury Mint
Dayton Hudson bears (some better)
Effanbee
Fisher Price (only great classic toys in great condition)
Franklin Mint
Gund
North American Bear Company
Raikes (a few better)
Star Trek (first series are the best)
Unused models (vehicles, airplanes, and trains)
Vermont Bears (some better)

Better:

Anchor Toy Company
Antique and vintage chess sets (the more unusual the better)
Barbie dolls (1970s or earlier)
Barbie clothes with tags (1970s or earlier)
Classic toys from the 1960s and 70s
Comic book items from the 1960s or earlier
Erector sets (vintage or antique)
GI Joe action figures (older)
Hot Wheels
Lego sets (vintage only)
Madame Alexander Dolls (older dolls)
Star Wars (those from the original movie are best)
Steiff stuffed animals (newer)
Strauss Bears

Best:

Action figures (in mint condition and in the box from the 1950s through the 1980s)

Annette Himstedt
Antique and vintage circus-related items
Antique metal toys (especially those made in Germany)
Antique military toys (metal)
Cast iron banks (Be careful of fakes!)
Hubley
Lawton
Lehmann
Lionel Trains
Marbles (antique or design made)
Mark Matthews designer marbles
Nancy Ann Storybook dolls (1940s–50s)
Richard Marquis designer marbles
Oaks
Schoenhut
Space toys from the 1950s and '60s
Steiff stuffed animals (antique)
Train-related toys (especially vintage and antique metal)

Gold Mine:

Antique French or German Bisque dolls (from the 1800s or earlier) such as Tete Jumeau, Steiner, or Belton
The original Barbie doll from 1959 in mint condition

Appendix 2
Helpful Websites

Art

http://www.askart.com/AskART/index.aspx

This website provides a comprehensive list of American artists past and present. It also provides a brief history about each artist and examples of his or her work.

Auctions

http://www.bonhams.com/us

The Bonhams and Butterfields website provides useful information about high-end auction houses. If you have a piece that you feel deserves to be sold at one of the premium auction houses, you can submit photos online. Your item must be worth at least $500, and you should be prepared to wait at least six weeks for a reply.

http://www.sothebys.com

Sotheby's also offers online assessments of your property that you may wish to sell. This website also provides a nice resource about auctions and antiques.

http://www.ebay.com

This is the home page for the eBay auction site.

http://auctions.yahoo.com

This is the home page for Yahoo auctions.

http://theauctionboard.com

This is an informational website about online auction news and resources.

http://www.auctionbytes.com/

This is a great informational website that has information about online auctions as well as articles about related topics such as antiques and collectibles. The site also offers a free newsletter.

Books

http://www.amazon.com

Amazon.com provides the most complete and comprehensive price guide for past and current books.

http://www.addall.com

AddAll's website allows you to search the web to find the best price for any book.

Collectibles

http://collectibles.about.com/

This is a great resource. It will take you to a web page that contains useful information about collectibles, and it also provides a wide variety of links to other websites that have information on specific collectibles.

http://www.disneyclassics.net/About_Disney_Classics_Collection.asp

This link takes you to a section of the Walt Disney Art Classics website, which provides great pictures and reliable information regarding a vast selection of modern-day Disney collectibles.

China/Pottery

http://www.replacements.com

The Replacements website is an excellent place to search for pattern names and prices on crystal, china, and silverware.

http://www.thepotteries.org/index.htm

Thepotteries.org is an excellent and detailed website about English pottery and pottery in general. It provides interesting history, terminology, and pottery marks.

http://www.pottery-english.com/

Pottery-English is another very good website that covers English pottery. This website is more selective than thepotteries.org is, but it has history on some of England's most famous potters. It has pottery marks for Wedgwood, Stafford-shire, Worcester, and others.

http://www.onlinecollectibles.com/faq/capodimonte2.htm

This link takes you to a section of onlinecollectibles.com that provides a history of Capodimonte Porcelain as well as pictures of the company's pottery marks, including dates the marks were used.

http://www.porcelainsite.com/porcelain/marks/

Porcelainsite.com is a very good resource for foreign porcelain marks.

http://www.porcelainmarksandmore.com/0pages/notes.php

This site provides additional information about porcelain, including tips on how to spot fakes and reproductions. It also provides additional references for porcelain marks.

Crystal/Glass

http://www.replacements.com

The Replacements website is an excellent place to search for pattern names and prices on crystal, china, and silverware.

http://1st.glassman.com/

This is a great website that features photos of antique glass as well as limited but very informative articles about glass.

Dolls

http://www.noramcneil.com/index.html

Nora's Antique dolls and Collectibles' website provides a limited but helpful look at antique dolls and doll clothing. The information may be limited but the pictures are excellent.

http://collectdolls.about.com/library/blmenu3.htm

This link is a vast warehouse of other web links to all kinds of dolls and doll-collecting information. It takes a good deal of time to sort through all the information, but you should be able to find a link to the information you are seeking.

Jewelry

http://www.am-diamonds.com

This is a great website where you can educate yourself about the color, cut, clarity, and carat weight of diamonds, but ignore the site's sky-high pricing structure.

http://www.oldeuropeandiamonds.com/index.html

The Old European Diamonds website has some interesting and informative information about old cut diamonds and other gemstones.

http://www.gemstone.org/gem-by-gem/gem-by-gem.html

This is a link to a page on the International Colored Gemstone Association's website. The page provides detailed information about a wide variety of gemstones. The photos are limited but overall this page is very informative.

http://www.bernardine.com/gemstones/gemstones.htm

Bernardine.com is another great website that has a section on gemstones. I like this site, because it has great pictures of both the cut and uncut stones.

http://southwestaffinity.com/

This is a great site for finding Southwest jewelry hallmarks and general information about Southwest jewelry and other items. Browse through the information links on the lower left side of the home page if you are interested in learning about jewelry made in the southwestern United States.

http://antiques.about.com/od/vintagecostumejewelry/
Vintage_Costume_Jewelry.htm

This is a link to a page that offers a nice selection of costume jewelry websites.

Mailing/Shipping

Before using one of the major private carriers, you should open an account with discounted rates based upon your expected amount of shipping. Links to the three major private carrier's websites (Fed Ex, UPS, and DHL) as well as to the United States Postal Service are listed below.

http://fedex.com/us/

http://ups.com/content/us/en/index.jsx

http://www.dhl-usa.com/home/home.asp

http://www.usps.com/

To use the United States Postal Service website, you will need to sign up online with a credit card. Priority mail boxes are free but in a limited number of sizes. USPS is great for small light weight items.

Silver, Sterling, and Pewter

http://www.modernsilver.com/basichallmarks.htm

This website provides a good general overview of sterling hallmarks.

http://www.silvercollecting.com

The Online Encyclopedia of American Silver Marks provides a list of the hall-marks of the major American sterling and silver plate manufacturers.

http://www.replacements.com

The Replacements website is an excellent place to search for pattern names and prices on crystal, china, and silverware.

http://www.silverwarehouse.com/

The Silverwarehouse website is a good place to search for pattern names and prices. The site is faster and easier to use than the Replacements website, but Silverwarehouse only lists the major American manufacturers and only shows pictures of the most popular patterns.

http://www.bhi.co.uk/hints/hmarks.htm

This link within the British Horological Institute website provides a very detailed list of the English sterling hallmarks. The site is somewhat difficult to use, but it is an excellent source if you do not have the ultimate book resource, which is *International Hallmarks on Silver collected by Tardy*.

http://www.925-1000.com/enyc_Overview.html

This is an excellent source of international and American sterling and silver hallmarks. It also provides date marks for Gorham and Tiffany silver.

http://members.aol.com/pewterpcca/Pewter Collector's Club of America, Inc.'s website provides hallmark identification and historical information about pewter objects. Go to the Introduction to Pewter Marks link from the site's table of contents for a great source on pewter marks.

Sports Memorabilia

http://www.psacard.com

Professional Sports Authenticator (PSA) is one of several major sports card and memorabilia grading companies. If you have a valuable piece of sports memorabilia, it may be worth the investment to have it authenticated and graded.

http://www.beckett.com/grading/

Beckett is one of several major sports card and memorabilia grading companies. If you have a valuable piece of sports memorabilia, it may be worth the investment to have it authenticated and graded.

http://www.sgccard.com/index.php

SportsCard Guaranty is not as well known as PSA or Beckett. The website has a rating scale from 10 (poor) to 100 (perfect).

Toys

http://www.antiquetoys.com

This website provides information on a wide range of antique toys.

Miscellaneous

http://www.freetranslation.com

This website is a valuable resource if you need to translate foreign words written on an item you are considering purchasing. Also, if an item has writing on it, and you do not know the country of origin, use this website to help you determine what language the writing is. That way you can determine the country of origin.

About the Authors

Daren and Nancy Baughman are cofounders of eBizAuctions, and they both live and work in Raleigh, North Carolina. eBizAuctions has been featured twice in *Entrepreneur Magazine*, and numerous articles have been written about the company in various newspapers.

Daren is a certified and licensed auctioneer, and he is also a Certified Purchasing Manager (CPM) with the Institute for Supply Management. He is from Allentown, Pennsylvania, and has been active in the auction and antique world from an early age.

Nancy is a Certified Personal Property Appraiser (CPPA) and a member of the Certified Appraiser's Guild. She is a native Texan with a background in corporate finance. Nancy gives seminars on how to buy and resell items as well as how to collect antiques.

Please visit Daren and Nancy online at their website www.ebizauctions.com to sign up for their free newsletter and to get information on their upcoming seminars and book signings.

978-0-595-42689-8
0-595-42689-1

Printed in the United States
128185LV00004B/166-213/A

9 780595 426898